THE THRONE OF RUBY AN ENDLESS EMERALD AFFAIR

Chronicle 26

Panagiota Makaronis

KREA PREA (TM). Est. 2012

The characters and events portrayed in this book are fictitious. Any similarity to real persons, living or dead, is coincidental and not intended by the author.

ISBN: 978-1-7641457-7-0

Cover design by: Copilot Panagiota Makaronis
Editor; KREA PREA (TM). 2012
Written; Australia Victoria Melbourne Craigieburn

I dedicate Chronicle 26 The Throne of Ruby an Endless Emerald Affair to the Corporate world; you are one of many;

The true Corrupt in society.

The reason why Humanity has no serenity an Industry that needs to be evaluated & exempt.

May your Body, Soul, Burn in Hell & your Spirit Linger to Rectify the Damages you Create to your Fellow man!

AMEN

When they cease the day & press replay.

The corrupt like follow up on another starting date they create. The confirmation starts with a validation, then followed up with a united front.

A Conspiracy to leave you wondering what did you do to deserve such a serve? What are they covering up, to catch up?

Forcing such a dark cloud over your shoulder. Just to have you tread carefully & trap he who used you to condition the mission; then avoid a confrontation.

Conspiring with the weak, to cover up the bleak. Assuming the end result will bring forth Peace.

Time, to let go & follow up on another show. Create a war in the Corrupts method once & for all.

Look within with no doubt, the rest will cease the day; under siege, with surveillance. It is part of a trend, that will give you shivers, within a cycle of reverence.

A reversed course of action that was rehearsed that served its purpose; with a curse.

An ending that was Pending;

An Endless Emerald Affair, Glorified with Truth & Dare!

PANAGIOTA MAKARONIS

CONTENTS

INTRODUCTION

The Throne of Ruby an endless Emerald Affair of Glory, Chronicle 26; a challenge I could not resist. It gave me power; an energy to persist. Not only I could see, the reality to that treaty, kick in. I wanted to return, kick a fuss, and kick he in the head; who attempted to sabotage me, to get ahead.

I felt trapped and wanted to kick them out, restraining with an order; all so they never return. A wish that has been pending for as long as I can remember. For I fell into a trap, became a victim, of scrutiny and a cover up. I had to reason with he who knew and he who created the piece.

I had to remain silent, avoid contact; to undo their creativity. I knew I was targeted by the corrupts, final coverup. One false move I would be stuck, trying to get out of a dead end and a death threat. It handed them a reason, to rush every momentum possible. It was the only way; they would let it go.

I hit a hold up; It gave me the power to redo, replace, and feed off the clue; left to the imagination. I was trying to come to terms with the fact it was a petty threat. Purely for the corrupt to cover up the fact they were stealing from petty cash. Hostage by an energy; that served a purpose.

Warned of what was to come from that outcome; had me on the Waiting list. A clue had been ruled, a return for one more review had come. A concept that was truly entertaining. It got to the point; no point taken. I was trying to avoid an enigma, to that dramatic effect; created by the corrupt defects.

Avoiding the issue was forming a truce, it gave me a chance to follow it up. Who, when, where and why created the mess. For he who was hired to hit back; confessed; then ran and hid. Assuming that will change their luck. It gave me the opportunity to return and feed off that rude awakening.

The corrupt were on my raider, ending there method periodically. It created a war in their peace leading them to a destination no longer lending them power to return and prosper; only ponder. An attempt to hit run, will bring forth a joyful event; a test that will hand me power to prevent them.

Because they covered their tracks well; it gave them a chance to pretend. No validation worth the allegation, for they delegating to be heard. A failed attempt, by he who knew and he who wanted to follow it through. He guessed wrong, and the assumption pestering me; became my redemption.

A damnation to the confession, lost the strength to carry on. Giving me the impression the mission was delayed for no reason. It handed me the competition to undo and uncover the plan. My method was not that simple; they could not see the light. They hit a hold up, just to hand them a screw up.

I hit an everlasting trace; a choice was made to erase that ongoing test. It had me foreclose another conquest, equivalent to a trace, that had me on the edge; ready to embrace. I had to cease the day, follow up on a journey so I can press replay. Forced to hit back with remorse; a rebellion effect.

In case I had a missing component; that was pending. I could not review nor undo, unless I gave in fed off the concept from within. I was to return and skip the corrupts method, leaving them entertained with the notion they won. In fact, it ousts them out quick; quieting my thoughts.

It handed me a key, allowing me to feed off their unity. For what I thought was a never-ending battle, in fact was the end of that trend. It had me forbode another road. So, when I reach the end of that task, I could undo that review and prepare myself for another accomplishment.

Where in the end of the fiasco, the vision was presented with a resolution; forsaken from that invasion. I was to release that beast, so I can advance with ease; as I process another request. After what they did to get to where they are. I could not careless if they never progress.

I had to prepare for a competition, a darkened vision; by the corrupts finally. It left me gnarly. I was on the other end feeding off that trace. It handed me a final challenge; consistent and consciously aware of the outcome. An energy left behind, saw me as an easy task and relatable; while sustained.

Facing them here, will be my way of feeding off them

all the way. A redemption to that damnation, that held me accountable. It became part of a test that forced the corrupt one again to confess. I was to hit back with treason for a bloody good damn reason. That was to return and test their patience.

An easy task, had come my way; this time around I could press replay. I come out the other end, forced to hit back, break the chain; no longer facing a dead-end. A lesson lived and well deserved. A desire to break the corrupts infatuation; to my destination. Creating a brand-new manifestation.

I heaved, for the shock to the system, served me a presentation. Because I was hit, in the end of that final bend. It created a war in the corrupts peace, handing me the evaluation to push them off the edge, straight into final a faith less vital. A journey less likely for them to repeat; I to remain silent.

I was sweetened by the game once again. Because the journey caved in on me way to early. There were several on my raider, waiting for me to enter freely. But little did they know, I was long gone. I made my mark; there was no way I was returning; to hit the corrupt heresy.

It was all part of a past, request that did not fall through. Because my journey changed, I survived it all the same. Whatever they attempted to achieve, became my way of accepting the facts. I was hit with foul play; for the wrong reasons. Obviously to reaccommodate a failed trend.

It became the corrupts way of achieving another bad day. I accomplishing a goal that served me well. I tried to outdo another review, and follow up on one more feast. Before I catch up, and feed off the concept and the corrupt try their luck to screw me up. I was on the other end asking for an encore.

I caught up, the comments froze, the corrupt were silent. They got caught cheating then tried to cover it up with a friendly meeting. That is when I knew I hit a hold up. It made me question their motive. Were they planning a new trick? Was I ready trade in treat them with a kind heart; a king hit.

All I knew, I hit check mate, and no comment from he who tried. He hit hold up for he got caught up; ran and hid. A given chance to advance and finalise the outcome to my favour. If they truly gave in; only time will tell. There was no easy way out nor freedom for them to return and hand me doubt.

I was not going to allow them to return or let my guard down either; unless it ended in my favour. I was way to profound and experienced with that method. It served me well and the purpose in the end was a waste of time. It purely created a diversion to push me off track.

He who conducted the trace had me facing a trend. In the end, with lady luck on my side; they hit a dead end. It forced me to rely on my spirit to get by. I truly believed those who played the fool took it too far. Nowhere near, where they were meant to be; the trust was a curse you cannot reverse.

Nevertheless, the corrupt were now irritated, forced to confess; for that method backfired. Back to where we were, before they tried to tie up a knot and create a cover up with a flaw. Assuming attacking me will help them rise and I fail; Handing them the Holy Grail.

Another lie, uncovered; just I can get the truth.

Amen.

CHAPTER 1

◆ ◆ ◆

WHEN YOU RETURN A FAITH; LESS LIKELY TO ERASE

I was led to release, then trace a challenge that was charmed. Where the conviction had me troubled. Where every time I was handed another violation to that destination, I was served a presentation. Where my energy flowed, survived, and brought me forward; straight into a prize.

So, when I hit the end, I was prepared, for a pause and effect. Where the only thing that forced me to win, was the last thing that had me enter the unknown. It was part of a follow up that led me to release force my way through then without further more create an encryption to that description.

Conditioning the mission, so I can follow up on another competition. Had me facing another wandering eye. t led me to believe that every trial and error was a pointless affair. It gave me the energy to finalize that trap that forced me of track.

For that restoration, was part of a manifestation. Recreating a faith, less likely for me to rejuvenate. Where my energy was stalled, it took me on a path that had me reaching my potential. I had no time than the present to repeat a trace to that case. It had me causing a mistaken, release to that piece.

A trap to that test, took me in and overlooked another theme. For that scheme had brought shame to my name. Instead of just letting go I made it worse, by chasing the curse. For I so wanted it to reverse. I was facing a destiny worse than the resurrection it had me facing another deception.

So, when I reached my next move. My faith had turned against me; I lost the will to survive a dive less likely to come alive. Because the corrupt had me tracing their lives, deciding my destiny. Waiting for me to come around and fight them so they can continue to come alive.

Because I fell and my journey had taken a wrong turn. It led me towards a direction that had me repeat another resurrection. I lost my way; I could not face, nor force my way in. Every trace had a challenge, that had me prepared for a win. Bombarded with negative thoughts from within.

I was brought forward then to my knees; on the condition I lose my position. With every, trace I had to finalize another test. The rules were broken and I was left outspoken. Forced to return for one more ongoing, and upcoming flaw. For what I was handed had me step into an extensive threat.

It gave me the proposal I needed to reach my peak, and lead the corrupt to a point of no return. It left me heated, terrified, and conceded, where the only way through had forced me to skip, escape, and trap a beat. Every trace took me in, finalizing that method from within.

For what it was worth, they could not let go, get through, or even take that praise. For I was handed a threat, that led me towards paying off a debt. Handing them a failed concept to that content. A presentation that had me convinced that the only thing left was the trace that had me content.

It forced me to repeat, overcome a cheat sheet, release a feast that had me repeat. I had to refine and hand the corrupt another time. It lined me up for a cause and effect, led on, and pushed off the edge. Trapped in the middle of a trend. It had me embark in a brand-new case; breaking the silence.

I had to cease the day and follow up on a vision. It forced me to release a competition; comparison to a mission. It had me fight for what I believed in. All while I process take that test hand the corrupt a confession a progress to the next final test.

I had to press replay, defending my honor all the way. Because the journey was humble, it had me facing another trace in the end of that turn of events. Forced me to reclaim another division to the game. A competition, based on a task that had me remain strong at last.

Because I was led astray, I had to portray another development along the way. I was not aware I hit a dead end to that trend it had me face a final trace. Giving me the power to undo and devour all while I divide conquer and survive another trace to that case that met me half way.

For my existence had me replace with persistence. Chasing me so I suffer in silence. All while I bloom in the mist that had me on the go chasing every flow. Without losing the momentum and myself included. I was forced to return for another cause reaching my potential at every force.

I hit a trace that had me on the edge, about to repeat and replace another case. It was part of a presentation to that destination that had me forgive those who had me locked in expecting me to lose that trend in the end. Facing me when I hit a dead end.

Where the only thing that led me to fail another win. Was causing an effect, it gave me a second chance to develop my innocence again. I was put in a position advised to hit back with a proposition. Where the only thing that come to be was the last thing that warned me.

I had lost my journey from within trapped in the middle of a trace. It had me face another cause and effect. It had me chasing the wrong dream, because I was put in a position worse than the mission. Where the troubles were to review; handing me another upcoming clue.

I had to release that beast, that faced me at the end of that feast. So, when I hit the end of that reservation, I pay for that terrible lie that got me through. Where I had to develop a new spell so when I reach my pinnacle it will save me and serve me well.

A release that saved me, warned me the feast was part of a cultural indifference. It forced me to reclaim another division to the game. A well-deserved desired key that gave me chance to belt the corrupt with unity. It had me face another case, cause an effect get back on track and resurrect.

Harming he who harmed me, leaving them all suffering in silence and dignity. All so I can rise above that fall, and harm who; when I hit that upcoming clue, a key. It was part of a spell that served me well, within reason. Without losing the one thing that brought me justice from within.

I was on my trace, looking for the end of that trend, that served me a whole lot good-deed. What good did it do though; only time will tell. All I knew is I was taught a lesson and the goal I set to achieve had me forced to repeat, replace, and push me off the edge; while I made my mark.

Even though the thought had me challenged, what come of it; was not what I was expecting. It was part of a trace, that had me pending for more. The debt was accumulating, all while I was stating the wrong facts. Creating a back track of energy that threw me a pack of lies; that served me a lead.

Where I was given an expense that had me trapped, ready to hit back with a vendetta. I could not hold back, even if I tried my thoughts were torn and my hard head was ready to tear apart those who decided to run a mile. Breaking my sorrow, leaving me living in silence.

I was losing my cool, I could not see the edge. I had to foreclose another trace, at the end of that case. I had to come to terms with the fact that the trace had me repeat replace and follow up on a trend that served me well in the end. Because I fell into a trip down memory lane.

I was taught a lesson; it left me on the edge returning for moral support. For I had one more pledge, before I hit the edge, where every trace brought me forward. It led me to believe that there only thing that had me back on track was the one thing that brought me back.

It was part of a trend that led me to release that beast. It forced me off the edge, all so I can find peace, repeating what I thought was the last resort. The beginning of a new raid that had me face another bad day. Had come and gone where I got in and replaced it with a new beginning.

The one thing that brought me forward, straight into a road of deception. It handed me the redemption to reclaim another competition. Putting the corrupt through hell, so I can win another storm to that faith. It had me resume the end of that trait with a constant reminder I fell into a trial.

It was part of a travel less likely for me to see the light. For the corrupt were on my raider, trying to follow up on another fight. I had to reprieve, another jealousy to convey then convince the corrupt every step of the way. Where every trace had me facing another case.

I was stuck trying to get out of a dead end, that had me fishing for one more trend. It was serving me well, hinting to me the corrupt were about to put me through hell. So, I decided enough was enough time to hit back with a royal flush. Force them to repeat and face them at every meet.

So, when the time come the energy that created the piece, forced me to release. I was trapped trying to follow up on another key. For those who endure to release that beast, had faced me at the end of that lease. Where I got in and had me overcome another outcome.

No time than the present, to release that feast, that forced the demon to reclaim its mission. It was part of a cycle of events that had me facing another tradition. It was part of a trace to that case, that served well. It gave me a second chance to evolve, while I invade in the corrupts final fantasy.

That final win, handed me peace. It created a dead end

in the end of that trend. It caused an effect and put the corrupt through hell, raising the dead. It had me releasing that demon that served me well. It led me to success, and a violation to that vision; that helped me win that competition.

Trapping the corrupt at every disposal, had me stating a new story. It was praising those who warned me. Feeding off those who forced me off the edge; straight into a ditch. It became part of an enigma. I was stuck living a lie just to catch the corrupts failure; a trace to that case the fed me.

Whatever had come my way, became part of an invite. It served me the last bite, evidently. For I was on the move and the corrupt were unavailable. Stuck in a trace, about to repeat and rebel against that forthcoming spell. It forced me up the hill down that pathway that led me astray.

For the corrupt had me return for another haunt. It had me stepping into a bad day. I was told to reveal that everlasting trace, it had me on the urge of creating a trend. I was torn in every direction led on, straight off the deep end. They made sure I lose my path and hit a final wrath.

It was anchoring me; I hit the end of that trend that led me face another case. It served me a trial an error and warned me of what was to come from that outcome. It gave me a final faith, before I hit the end of that trace. For whatever forced me to release that beast; gave me a chance to release.

For that beast that forced me to find peace, had me releasing a new thought, where I get in and repeat a new win. Where I go for one thing and that was to create a follow up towards another destination. A trace that had me tested had caused an effect and had me trade in for new review.

It forced me to get in and finalise that presentation that had me roaming. I had to finalise that trace that led me to repeat and rebel against those who faced me. It forced me to delete, delay, and try my best to confess, follow up on a request. What was to come from that outcome; was interesting.

It had me facing another dilemma, it led me to repeat, delete delay, and follow up on a game. It had me press replay. For what I knew and what was to come from that review had me facing another clue. The trace at the end of the race that had me causing an effect, warning me; I wasted nothing.

I had to break the silence as I resurrected, for every momentum had me in admin. I was ready and willing to preach the good the bad and the willing; just to pay out another debt. For the condition took over the mission it had me convinced that every trace was forcing me; to release the beast.

For that method had pushed me off the edge, praising the corrupt at every tread. It had me feeding off the thought that had me hit the last resort. I was given a reason to repeat and rebel against the corrupts position.

A current investigation had come and gone.

I was given a written report to feed off the outcome. I was so caught up with a trace where the energy that had me facing another case caused an effect. I was taught a lesson creating a piece that had me release. For every trace created a trend and every follow up caused an effect.

It had me releasing a test that forced me to resurrect. I had to revive another knot, just so I can catch up and get by. I had to feed off the trend that had me break the silence in the end. Starting again was not part of the game though it led me on and faced me again.

Because my passion, caved in on me; it brought me peace. For every time I was trying to get back on track and feed off the impact. I was served well it forced the corrupt through hell. There was something in the air, that had me follow up on another verse; ready and willing to cause an effect.

CHAPTER 2

◆ ◆ ◆

A FINAL REVIEW BEFORE I RETURN FOR AN ENCORE

I had to skip those who knew, because apparently their hypocrisy was part of a final review. Where I spoke in tongue, just to cave in on the concept, because I was done. It had me pleasing the corrupt in the long run. I was given a challenge that had me replace another case.

It had me forced to hit back with a pointless affair. Facing a trace that ended the case. I was on the road to recovery, where every journey forced me to hit back with a rumour. A curse that led me towards a trial an error, a challenge that served me trap. Lining me up for a curse I could reverse.

For those who caved in on the concept, had no reason to hit back. I could return, release the beast cause an effect and find peace; within treason. All in one setting, for I had to face a trace, so when the time come, I could create a better understanding to what I did to deserve such an outcome.

I thought it was part of an everlasting concept. It had me forced to hit back with remorse. All while I kicked a fuss, for the corrupt had it in for me way to early. They took me in and finalised that method as if their life was worth living. It had me in admin hitting a home run.

It was to bring forth, what I assumed was part of their commune. In fact, they fell and I reached my pinnacle looking forward to the next trace. It was part of a trend to break the cycle and feed off the energy that had me forced to pretend. In the end entertainment and energy wasted was uncovered.

It had me forced to hit back, torn in several directions. It was a trace that tested my patience, and listed the corrupts trend. A method that served me a key, and led me towards a destination where I hit the end of that reservation. I was let go; it had me preventing the corrupt from re-entering.

I had lost my freedom my key was discerning, it had become part of a trial an error. An informative trend that belted the corrupt in the end became obvious. I was oblivious, it had me Returning and jumping the gun again. Relisted, a new key recreated a trace that served me a trial and error.

It was a follow up to the next terror, just so I can skip he who was following me. Forcing me to release the beast and follow up on another feast. It had me catching up creating a fuss forcing the corrupt to hit a robust. So, when I hit the dead end it was the end, I got in no longer pretending.

For the last resort, that restored my energy. It taught me how to remain in the game, and regain conscious awareness again. I was hit with a threat, and it returned with a turn of events. It served me well; it presented me with an expense. I was hit with a threat to an exit; where I evacuated.

I was serving the wrong, feeding off the pathway; that had me sitting at the bench. I was waiting to be called up my patience ran thin I could not wait anymore. So, I forced myself to hit back, repeat, repel face another method while I create a forthcoming spell.

Before I hit the trace, it forced me to repeat another warning. It taught me a lesson and fed me a whole lot of exposure, heaving at me while I release that feast. It forced me to undo and create another clue. I had no force to hit back with remorse. It had me redo and accomplish another clue.

It led me to repeat repel and put the corrupt through hell, just to face another challenge. All while I hit back with an expense, where the silence hit the end of that trend. It had me repeat another good deed. For what I thought was part of the last resort, had me facing another aroma.

A constant reminder I hit a decipher. It was part of a scheme, that hit me and knocked me out on between. Not only I was put in a position where I was evolving, but there was no trace no case no condition to replace. It was part of a key that had me repeating and relying on the corrupt to get by.

For every journey, I was put on was a joke. Not only I was let on, led astray, I became delusional all the way. It was part of a given, a challenge that was forbidden but handed to me anyway. It gave me a trace that handed me the cause an effect; releasing that demon so I can resurrect.

It was part of given. where the corrupt took me in; faced me then trapped me. It ruined my destiny from within. I was fighting for an entrance that had me serving a differentiation to that manifestation. It caused an effect and handed me the road that lined me up for a test.

I could not follow up on a trace, all because the corrupt were avoiding me. Hoping I will fall fail and I lose my identity. I entered a passageway towards a journey that led me astray. I was taught a lesson left to repeat release that dead end. Forced the corrupt to undo and revive a forthcoming clue.

There was tear, in each direction I had no time to sow it up. I had repeat it, take each piece, and attach it to the new, from the old. Because each lesson had me reach my destination. Preaching my truth and trapping those who hit back. I was forced to finalise the lead, by overlapping that twist.

Where each patchwork became part of my research. For every journey saw me as a threat, and the only way I could return for a better outcome was tread carefully. I was to enter the unknown with a prediction that had me on the edge. Restoring my energy, feeding off the trace a force to replace.

All while I hit the corrupt consciously. Breaking the system finalising that test that had me process it all. It was part of an affair that forced me toward progress. Feeding on the success not off it. Because I was offered a key, and left to hit back with unity. When the time come return then repeat.

As I was to cause an effect and rebel against the outcome. It gave me a chance to hit the corrupt with a trend, it served me well in the end. Before I was to hit back and feed off the impact, I was handed a final. It had me on trial, a second time around; a hit that led me towards a trend.

It faced me with a new brand, an intense debt that brought me forward straight into a final threat. A challenge that taught me a lesson and created a final uproar. Before I was to return and hit the corrupt with a threat. A task that took me in and finalised that method; that forced me to give in.

Handing the corrupt a failure to launch, had me winning a fight. It forced me to repeat rebel reappeal; while I send them a token of my imprecation. Just to cancel the corrupts method, look into that trace that forced me to replace hand me the incantation to that final manifestation.

A perfection to that presentation, became part of my feast. It had me step forward into the next release. I was handed a test left to process all the information. So, when I hit the end of that faith that had me forced to enter. I was given a chance to hit back and watch the corrupt surrender.

It led me towards a journey that will bring me forth. Line me up for another cause, it took me for a ride that served me a challenge. I was faced, me with a curse I could reverse. If only I could undo and review another eye opener, that left me forced to undo.

For the corrupt had undertaken another fake and false reading. They took me in and forced me to reclaim another division to the game. It had me on the move gambling that troubled momentum. All so I can continue to reap a reward and follow up on a torn event that served me a trace.

I was hit at the end of the case with a follow up. It had me presenting the corrupt with a challenge to remain the same. I was fed a whole lot of drama, it held me up, and foolishly held me in. It consumed my every ounce of energy, to that redemption that had me failed a classification.

A contest to that everlasting quest, was a challenge, it helped me embrace a case. So, when I caught up, I could request a new test. Because I was put in a position that served me a proposition it landed me a role that took me on a path. A follow up, that had me requesting another trace to that case.

I was taken for fool left to remain silent, all while the rest hit back with a quest. It had me release that feast that served me a new lease. Then when the time overcome another outcome. I was fed off from within. It was part of case that had me face another trace.

It took all my power, to follow up and devour; all while I divide and conquer. I was forced to hit back with remorse, feed off the trick that led me to release the beast. A key that caved in on the concept and presented me with closure. I was served a disclosure, that manifested beyond my control.

It took me on a journey, without reasonable doubt. I was taken on a path that had me wrong all along. For those who overrode me and served me a treat; were creating a chaotic effect. It had me forced to hit back, repeat, delete delay then hand the corrupt a warning.

There was no time to scheme for a new theme. Only a trace that handed me a case that caused an effect; breaking the corrupts free ride. It was serving me well and heaving at me while I went through hell. Not only I was given a chance to advance; I was set alight with a with an assumption.

I was given a reason to undo that corrosion, from a confused archaic confession. It had me reaching an everlasting conclusion. It had me confused, left to delete delay and deny the corrupt access all the way. For I was given a resurrection to that manifestation that hit me at the end of that trend.

Because I was trying to stay afloat, the anxiety took over my reality. I had to drift into my own thoughts, so the corrupt could return and finalise that trace that had me ongoing. I was ready to replace, recreate a trend that took me on a path about to regret was I was set out to achieve.

It left the corrupt to delegate to that next trait, and I was also given an opportunity to rise above and beyond the corrupts final adversity. Handing me the conclusion that every confession was part of the corrupts delusion. It had me embrace and follow up on another informative case.

A trace that will hand me a curse so I can reverse, became evident. I was taking my time stalling for one reason and that was to give in and hand the corrupt another favour to win. All while the corrupt debate and follow up on another key. Giving me the power to override another ungrateful event.

An outcome that will help me come first, had me cease the day; forced me to press replay. Then when the energy saw me easy, it caused an effect and created an expense that had me forced to hit back with remorse. I had felt a dark cloud come over my thoughts; the feeling was roar.

I was to hit back with an encore. For the corrupt were competing with me. Compelled by the sound, I was taken for a fool and left to hit back profound. For the sound that had me facing another trace was hitting the corrupt at the end of the race. Because they worked in unison, I had to fight back.

I was on my own knowing I had no back up; to stand my ground. They found that I was to brave and they decided to work in unison to teach me a lesson. I was given a test, and left to be strengthen my soul on the condition I reap another reward. I was handed a review to follow up on another clue.

For they had me stating a fact creating a war to get back on track. It had me forced to hit back with remorse. It led me towards a journey where I was handed a clue. It had me reap a reward and create a challenge that served me well and pushed me forward straight into hell.

For there was no way, I could undo that review, nor follow up on a forthcoming event. Unless I hit the corrupt with a brand-new threat. The evaluation was part of a competition, where the corrupt were to be examined. Then scrutinized for their work, just to hit the end of that trend.

A trace that had the corrupt state a new fact, created an anomaly; all so I can get back on track. It had me reach my peak and create an expense that had me hit back with a curse. It forced me to rehearse and reveal another upcoming event. For the corrupt reached their limit.

I was on the move, reluctantly playing the game. It was way past the trace, where the key was replaced. I found a way to break the corrupts spirit, feed off the method and lead me astray. I had no freedom to face another trace; I was handed a key to follow up on a new review.

I had to doubt, the trace, to track down the corrupt; caused an effect. It had me force my way in, and break the cycle. For that bad taste in the back of my mind had me case close that test. It forced the corrupt to return for a plea bargain. Finally, each task had me righteous; fighting for my life.

It saw me easy; it caused an effect had me resurrect. It was to clear the deck and hand me another trace to that case. It led me to believe I had no freedom nor foundation to reprieve. I had one thing to overlook and with pleasure, it handed me a key feeding off the corrupts industry.

Where their insecurities took over, I hit the end of that trend. Forced me to repeat, then take the road to the next request. Undoing an inconclusive event; holding me back. I had to relay a resentful event, where the gamble took me in and recreated a new tread in the end of that trace.

It served me well in the end, I had to force my way in and fiercely take the initiative. All while I belt the corrupt from within. It was handing them the outcome that I need to follow up on. A trace that broke that cycle, that had me force my way in and finalise that method from within.

At the end of that forthcoming thread, I had to face another trace; just to release that relentless case. It was part of a case to erase a challenge that took me further. It had me following up on another method and praise whom ever, just to hit back and hand me a treasure.

While I hunt for a new improved creative move. I was given a reason to follow up on another treason. It was part of a pointless affair that warned me I had erase that trend. It pushed me off the bend, straight into a troubled event; that had me on the edge.

It was a challenge, that had me face another trace. It was the only way I could prevent the corrupt from harming me again. A pathway towards resurrection. Where every journey served me a pulse and every trace and had me erase a curse on impulse. It was handing me a chance to reverse.

All while I rehearse another trip down memory lane. For every case, had me refrain from reliving the same game. A nightmare, that took over that dynamic that was causing an effect. It became part of a campaign that had me remain, simple minded. I had to refrain from reliving a hoarse to that cause.

It had caused and effect and faced me with another, defect. A warning to follow up on a past test the brought me a faith I can detest. I was ready to replace the old start new and feed off the concept. It gave me the upper hand to screw he who knew, breaking the silence.

I was working towards a challenge that had a me waiting for a clue. I could not compel, against the will of those who put me through hell. I could not comprehend what the challenge had installed. Because I was kept in the dark, waiting patiently for the corrupt to state a new fact.

It had me facing another trace, it led me towards a journey that had me passing tests. Then handing keys to those who had nothing better to do unless I handed them a clue. A trend that served me a wrong move, forced me to hit back with an ongoing review.

Where in the end of that trend I had no freedom to pretend. It was a waste of time, it caused an effect and had me hit back with a prerequisite. It was to break the silence and force me to pretend. For every trace that caused the effects had me resurrecting.

Meanwhile the corrupt were protecting one another. Hoping I would fall fail and lead the pact towards a destination that will hand them resurrection. Infect that was far from the truth It had me roaming for more clues; a challenge I could review. For what I could deliver, served me well.

It handed me the freedom I needed to go through hell. For that one thing that was part of the desire. Handed me a review, to finalise the concept and escape presenting the corrupt with an immoral dilemma. A Grand entrance to that next turn of events.

It Had me waiting for an edge, so I could pledge. Discarding the cause, had me facing another waste of prediction it caused an effect and handed me a brand-new evaluation. because the dream was so harsh to analyse. The dramatic effect took me on a path of creating an override to that task.

Instead of bringing me peace and joy, it had delivered me a sentence. A failed attempt to hand the corrupt a challenge so I can resurrect. Handing the corrupt a chance to hit me with the wrong intention. A redemption that isolated the truth, it took over the trace and handed me a guess...

CHAPTER 3

◆ ◆ ◆

HAND ME A GUESS & SET FREE FROM THAT REQUEST

Because, I needed to get back on track, the corrupt returned and hit me with an inquest. Testing the patience, of those who repeat. With a trial an error and a final vendetta. I was to repeat replace a trace; at the end of that case. Return and restore a method; where they tested my patience.

I had to refine, then reserve another warning to that desired effect. I was on the edge of creating a new pledge. Where every journey faced me, with a test a desired request. It was giving me the impression I hit a conquest. I had to deny the corrupt access to a challenge that had me threatened.

For every desired effect was a lie. I was on the move trapped in the middle of a constant reminder of a past dilemma. For the corrupt had me cornered ready and willing to break the cycle. As if the trace broke the trend and forced me to release that final feast.

All so they can catch up feed off me at every assumption. For the challenge was to meet their quota where they were to take a break all by faking their death. Assuming they could release that beast forced me to undo and finalise that clue; creating an anomaly.

I had to reserve that atmosphere that had me sitting at the end of that trend. It caused an effect and faced me when I hit a dead-end. I had to release that beast that forced me to find peace. I was given a reason to embrace a treason. Accomplish a goal, while I remind myself, I hit a death threat.

I had to drag it on and force my way in. It had me feed off the concept, while I get back on track and condition the mission, following up on another vision. It had me presenting the corrupt with a trace a follow up on a case. Forcing me to repeat replace and present the corrupt with a warning.

They were dragging it on, assuming they would get back on track. But all it did was have me forward it to the next of kin. Separating the corrupts method, so I can get in and win another inning. It was part of a trend in the end of that trace. It had me causing an effect, with a dead-end lead in the end.

It was going back and forth, up, and down at every trace. It had me on the edge repeating another case. All while I catch up and fight for what I thought was the last resort. Because what I believed was part of a curse it served me well and presented me with an upcoming spell.

For that case caused the effects and created a defence. It made me see the reality, but sense that I hit a deception to that redemption. It had me face another fear follow up on a trend it gave me a second chance to hit back in advance waiting for the corrupt to follow up another trace.

I was used abused left to suffer in the corrupts conquest. All so I can see past the trust, trace that track that caused the effects it had me stepping into a trial an error. I had to follow up to the next tremor. Where the energy to condition the mission will stall; while the corrupt lose control.

All while prosper from that undeniable response. I needed to reclaim a conscious awareness to the game. It served me well at the end of that trend. It was feeding off the ongoing thought. But all it did was have me restore, repeat feed off the trace that forced me to delete.

So, when I reach my pinnacle, I could invade in the corrupts invertible trace. It had me facing another case. I had no faith and the troubles that took over, had taken its toll. It gave me a second chance, I was served a cancelation key, at the end of the race.

It was part of a foundation, that forced me to hit back

and feed off the trace. It was all over before it began. Handing the corrupt a dead end, giving me the power and the prediction to release all inhibitions. Ending the corrupts production. Because I was stuck in the middle of a trace.

I needed to follow up on a new trend, because I had an imposter in the mist. Had me on the edge facing another pledge. It was Impacting my moves feeding off the trace, haunting me at the end of the race. Trying to catch up and feed off me when I hit the end of that travesty.

They were twisting my words around, handing me the insecurity to follow up on a trace. I was given an impression, where I fell in to an enigma to that manifestation. What I needed to do to catch up; was force the corrupt to own up. I had to release that beast, a given chance to hit back in advance.

It forced me to overcome another outcome discreetly facing another role up. As if I was part of a trace that took me in and had me pending from within. I was on the mend, trapped in the middle of a forthcoming riddle. For what I knew and what was handed to me back then; was a failed attempt.

It was part a trap, to donate to the corrupts presentation. For apparently their investigation was part of a concept that led me to the next reservation. All so I can continue on my journey and investigate another trace to that case that caused effect. It had me revoked, handing me an evaluation.

I was taken for a fool, establishing the corrupts final entrance. I was on board, forced to hit back with remorse. Silently taken for a ride, facing a trace to that case. It caused an effect. I was reported and for that reason I was to hit back with remorse just to find peace. Because I was too courageous.

It had me presenting corrupt with a clue. Leading me to a destination that had me refined. Framing them for returning and hitting me all over again. An inclination to hand me a dead-end to that trend. It became part of a bribe. I had to follow up on a tribe just to catch up and feed off the corrupt.

It was failing me at every test, so I decided to give in feed off the trace. It had me intertwining with a trail an error and a final vendetta. It had me waiting for another entrance. A destination where others were competing with me. Even though I was staring destiny's Glow.

The corrupt still wanted to release that beast. It had me ongoing, feeding off the trace that served me a piece. A challenge that ended in what I thought was the last resort. Forced me to hit back and trace that impression. Presenting me with a key, that had me forced to hit back with remorse.

I was taken by surprise and forced to override a deception, to that allegation. It taught me a valuable lesson. It was part of a main event, and even then, that key became one hardcore reality kick. A game that pushed me off the edge, straight into a trap. Forced me off the trend; into a dead end.

It was part of a challenge that had me facing another bad day. A challenge that forced me to press replay. It had me returning to reclaim a division it had me revealing another competition. Where I divided, conquered, and fell into the deep; straight into to the narrow.

I was forcing the corrupt to give in and hand me a win. It was creating an expense, that served me an expose. A trend leading those who knew towards a journey that forced me to hit back with a review. It was facing the corrupt with a dead end at the end of that trend.

It was to face another curse, just to give the corrupt a chance to rehearse another verse. It was giving me the power and the energy to release. Where that final piece had me feeding off the concept so I can release peace. Handing me a terrible lie, that forced me to get by.

I had to divide and conquer, facing another trade. I was hit with a conspiracy, where the corrupt saw me easy. For my final days were met, and I was still standing waiting for the corrupt to hit back. Then own up, leaving them testing the patience of whom were reminiscing.

It had me facing a trend that was failing me in the end. Handing me the earth, a vital energy that I needed to release that feast. It forced me off the edge straight into a journey that led me towards a trial. It was causing effects and giving the corrupt a dead end in the end of that trend.

It was not part of a trend it was part of the corrupt

finals. An error that created a terror attack. Where I was in the middle of that terrible attack. It had me remain silent to the game guessing wrong so I can give in and feed off the mission from within.

My crown of Glory had burnt, and I had to repeat that final faith, it had me reach my pinnacle. Hitting the end of that tremor, with a final dilemma. Where that failed attempt had me ending one cycle and the beginning of another. It was feeding off the trace that had me replace another case.

For every trace that was handing me an opportunity, to release that beast. Forced me to repeat and follow up on another trap. It was giving me the indication I hit the end of that manifestation. Creating a piece that led me on and faced me in the long run.

It turned into a release, where I could reverse and find peace. I had to invite then validate another break. With a silent intake, finalising the trend; that hit a dead end. It had me reaching my peak and facing another trace to that case that caused an effect. It broke the silence and fed of that debt.

It took me in and freed me from within. I had to finalise the outcome, all so I can remain the same. Forcing me towards a level of trapping the corrupt at every final arrival. It was leading me towards a destination where the trace became a masking tape to a game that hit another level.

It was part of an integration that led towards an interrogation. It had me repeat and finalise that pledge.

It had me feeding off the trauma that pushed me off the edge. It was part of a pointless affair that took me towards another journey. Just to catch up find peace while I feed off the interest.

It had me release the beast, with an undeniable feast. A level of madness, I could not restore, had come to my attention that is when I knew I hit a redemption. Unless I picked up where I left off the energy that stated thew facts created an encore. An entrance to the unknown.

It had me feeding off an entity that had me release that beast that forced me to find peace. For those who forced their way in took the initiation as an assumption. Failing me from within where I get in and finalise that test that had me energised. Forcing my way through; feeding off the trend.

It had me pretend, I had to face another trace give in and fail the corrupt from within declining a fragment of my morbid imagination. A second chance to trap those who knew in advance. Then create a new key, then follow up on another theme. A scheme that will help me redeem.

I had to trace that curse that hit me with a verse. It gave me a second chance to cause an effect and lead the corrupt towards the right destination. Where the only thing that hit me from within was part of an investigation. For the trace that served me well at the end of the race; creating a piece.

So, when I hit the corrupt back with the same trace. It will become part of my treasure; it will have me engage in a tremor that will serve me well, handing me a warning. So, the corrupt can release A demon; served at the end of that trend. An energy that led me to face a revival to that deploy.

It had me surviving another trace to that case. Where this time around, I was taught a lesson let down and given a chance. Ti hit back with a minimal effect on my end. I had to get in and feed off that test that failed me when I hit the end of that request.

I had to force my way through fix the damages that had me repeat another review. It had me face another case, save he who hit me and ran. Just to get a glimpse of a trace that had me give in and feed off the treasure that forced me to repeat and press replay; finalising another bad day.

I was forced to hit back with a rebound at the end of that track. Where every trace faced a case, every verse turned around and hit me with a verse. Where the corrupts method backfired and I was returning forcing them to hit back and finalise that impact that raised the buck.

It created a challenge that had me fight back and stir the pot. Where the corrupt were to hit back with a verse, where they cannot reverse nor rehearse; because I returned and come first. For that final feast will hand me a key that will burn and bring me back to reality.

It will be the first and last time the corrupt will give in and feed off the crime. This time around the trace that broke the silence from within will give me a chance to belt the corrupt in advance. Where every trial will descend, every trace will bend and every final force; will service me well in the end.

I had to pretend that I was on the move, giving me the incantation to follow up on another manifestation. An interrogation that caused an effect, created a destination that warned me I hit the end of that trend. I had to release a desire, while I desert the next feast from that piece.

While I was given the freedom to return, for the last curse. Where the only thought that come my way was the one thing that had me press replay. For I what I was given and what was bound to happen. Was just a desire that handed me the power to undo and devour.

Giving me the opportunity to give in, had me step forward; following up on another win. It handed me the forbidden, a result that took me in and finalised that method so I can win. I had to follow up on a force that led me to repeat. An energy that had me step into a powerful effect; was on edge.

A desired result that deserved to be rejected; left to the imagination. Because the corrupt fell and handed me a verse, all so I can catch up and come first. It had me reaping a reward and taking the initiative, so I can claim my truth and feed off the corrupt. All while I step into the unknown.

I head west, hit south, return at east, caused an effect at North. Just to find myself in the middle of a constant reminder, that the trace was causing effects and creating, a defect. That led me towards a warning where every trace, that handed me a test. It led me towards a journey; I could not contest.

A feast that had me on the urge, repeating another surge. It led me towards a burn that took me in and ran me up towards another sin. It was part of a curse that led me towards a destination. Forcing me to repeat another restriction. I found that the entertainment was part of the corrupts basement.

Found myself nesting in the same domain, waiting for the corrupt to claim another informative game. Where my destination had me facing another allegation. That is when I knew I was pinpointing the wrong view, and define another trace to that case.

I was no longer pointing the finger at the wrong person. Because I found out the truth; my life had become quite interesting. I was left to retaliate, hit back and face the corrupt with the notion that their prediction was precious. The leisure was led to believe the trace was part of a case.

It had me repeating a trace, that turned into a lie. It gave me a chance to face the corrupt feed off the method undo that clue and break that silence. I was left facing another review. Trapped in a curse I could not reverse. Hitting those who hit me; leaving them regretting ever meeting me.

For there was no trace, it had me on the urge of breaking the silence. It had me feeding off what I thought was part of a test, that had me forced to hit back with remorse. For the curse had me come first, it was the beginning of a trend that had me face another ending; that was pending.

Where I gave in and fed off the trend that had me facing another dead-end. I was led to believe that every trace had no foundation nor freedom to breath. It was part of a defence, that had me fast forward and hit the corrupt at the end of that trend; forced me to pretend.

With one trace left, I was to hit back with a feast. Where the corrupt were supposed to lead me towards a journey that saw me easy. All so I can get back on track and feed off the trace that drew me closer from within. Teaching them a lesson finally; a trend that led me towards, the right path.

Where I can return the favour and fail the corrupt at last. It faced me with another failed attempt, a journey that will help me face another case. A challenge I could chew on, catch up, and review another clue. I was taught a lesson and left to enrage those who had me reaping rewards.

I had to engage and gamble in a trace, that served me well. It presented me with upcoming spell. Every time I went for a hit and run, it created a vital response; to that outcome. It a part of a trace that was versatile I hit an end that caused an effect and handed me an inspiration.

My potential had been scrutinised; it caused an effect and trapped me. I was given a reason to reclaim another trace to that case that caused an effect and brought me forward. It had me on the corrupts raider, lining me up.

A debate had opened, warning others on how and when
to harm me.

CHAPTER 4

◆ ◆ ◆

WHEN A TRACE BECAME PART OF TRIAL

Faced with a speculation, a step into the next destination. A rumour that forced me to return the favour. Where my creativity come to hold up, a point, where I had no end. I no longer needed to prove anyone anything; I was innocent. An analysis of my true self; came to an understanding.

It was handing me the evolution, to sustain and feed off the trace. It had me on the urge of repeating another case. I was taught a lesson forced to review and follow up on an entrance to entertain me at every violation. Stepping into the unknown.

Where every journey had me sustaining the one thing that had been remaining. A final force to that substance that sustained my true energy. Where I was given a reason to return with treason. I made it to the finish line where every line up was part of a final degree.

It handed me the evaluation to break the silence and feed off the trend; that passed me in the end. Breaking the corrupts train of thought was part of a cutting edge. A lead towards he who had a head start for he who used me to get ahead. For every superstition created a proposal of bad luck.

It had me facing a case, forced to replace with a trace. Based on a past offence, warning me I was being taught a lesson; on impulse. It became a fight so I catch up and finalise that trace that had me reaching my potential. I was rising above and beyond what I thought will keep me strong.

All while the corrupt were stringing me along. A theme that warned me I hit a failed attempt in-between. The whole concept that had me reaching my potential losing my lead. So, when the time come, I could follow up on another trend. A trace that will hand me the freedom to pretend.

It had me creating a concept, purely to attract the wrong. So, when I reached my potential, I hit a hold up where in the end of that trend. It became part of an everlasting dead-end. I was taught lesson it had me feed off trace that broke the silence in the end of that thread.

I had to retrieve and follow up on another breed.

Because the one who created the piece retired. The key was handed to the next of kin and I was their victim. It was part of a scheme that had me releasing another failed trace in-between. It was part of a final payout a gift that kept giving.

For he who knew took me in, purely to break my silence so he can win. I took it as an innocent challenge, but when I walked in the corrupt saw me easy. Forced me to hit back catch up ending that trace; pushing me off track. An energy interpreting it as a follow up; to hand me an award.

Because I achieved all my goals in the end, I was left to repeat rebel feed off the trace that put me through hell. Facing me at every honourable event, thanking me for the energy that took me in and presented me with a forthcoming win.

I honestly believed this was the end, and I got through. In fact, it was the beginning of another clue. The corrupt thought taking me in, and shocking me on a continuous basis will help them win. It was part of a trace that caused an effect and led me to believe a whole lot of lies.

For that energy that had me rise, gave me a challenge that will hit me when I was served a curse. It had me face another trace it gave me a chance to delve into a trace that served me a loyalty card and presented me with a feast that had me release that final piece.

For that journey, it forced me to win, it gave me a second chance to win. It handed me a curse, a trial an error I could rehearse. I was hit at the end of that verse. I had to rise and raise the buck just to catch up. So, when the time come the only thing that belted me from within was the trace.

The other part was uncanny, impatient and it became a force that hit me with remorse. It served me well. It presented me with upcoming spell; it had me face another day. It gave me a second chance to press replay. So, when I hit the edge the method it will space the corrupt out.

It gave me a second chance to pledge; it had me rise above and beyond. What I thought was part of a long-term memory, brought me joy, it handed me the drive to survive. Even though it was a lie, that was meant to come true. I did everything in my power to not tie that knot, or make it happen.

Because that method was not going to end in bliss. It was part of a tragic event, that had me stagnant to my development. For the corrupt were planning to harm me. It handed me short term memory. Stuck in a time warp; with silent treatment it led me to believe every angle served me well.

It forced me to repeat, rebel against he who took me in; and fed off me from within. It had me rise above and beyond, reaping a reward and feeding of those who were wrong all along. In fact, it had me stepping into a trace, that forced the corrupt to repeat, rebel erase while finalising that case.

It was the beginning of an ending; that was pending.

Handing me the urge to spray my venom. It was part of an urgent response to that cause an effect. It was disheartening, to see I was being had and the only way out was to get out of it and not show any concern.

For conditioning it the way it was stated by the corrupt handed me a hold up. Where the corrupt had a chance to press play. I had to let it go, so I can continue to follow up on another show. It was to teach the corrupt a lesson and repeat another competition.

One that had me sitting on the edge remaining silent. Meanwhile press delete delay and follow up on another day. A challenge that will hand me the joy to be able to remain stable. For I could not fight back nor could I find truth, because every trace had me uncover another sequence.

I was put in a position where the corrupt found me easy. They repeated the competition at the end of that mission. Where I was on my path, torn at every proposal, serving me a key that had me facing a final degree. For the task at hand was bland; I reached my pinnacle mastering my craft.

I fed off the trend that had me foretell another dead-end. Not only I was led on but I was put in a position where the corrupt kept leading me on. I replaced and uncovered up another rumour. Just to catch up, where my journey led me to undo another review; forced to release that beast.

I was to undo a new feast then when the time come

reveal an outcome. It was part of a key that led me to follow up on a lie then when the time come; reconsider. I had to relay, stick to the plan where every trace served me a case. For he who assumed he knew me well, took me in.

Assuming he who had the power to put me through hell. Could entertain me with the notion I had no freedom to hit back. Every trial took me on a path way; it handed me the freedom to hit back with a personal vendetta. A second trial that stirred the pot, with a trace to release that beast.

It forced me to repeat replace and continue on my journey as if I was out of place. I was stuck hitting a trace that handed me a bad taste. Where every time, I hit the end of that trend, I had to follow up on a new curse; Force my way in and break the silence from within.

It was part of a trend that served me well and presented me with a forthcoming spell. A challenge that will put me through a curse that will serve me well. It restored my energy and broke every trace that served me well. It put me through a journey that forced me to break the cycle.

I was on a path that was pending each trend was never ending. It was to repeat a reward force my way in breach a contract and face another win. It was part of a trend that fed off the ease that hit me at the end of that trace that caused an effect; facing me with a trial at the end of that debt.

I was stuck pausing effects and finalising that debt. Where every outcome served me a clue, it gave me the entrance to give the corrupt a chance to screw he who knew and break the silence of he who had a clue. For I needed to repeat then take a moment to press delete.

While I fake a trick and treat the corrupt as if that trend was starting a new. It gave me the free ride to break the silence and feed off he who knew. It was to pass a test, case the request and finalise that method so I can return and request another test. It was to please me until the end.

All while I face, he who conditioned the mission, where every tradition, took me on a pathway where I lost my way and the only way to cover up a challenge was reserve the corrupts method and hand them another bad day. Where the omen of that trend, had covered up another dead end.

A trace that handed me a dead end, it took me on a path way; where I had to pretend. It had me repeating a challenge, it restored an energy so I claim another division to the game. Just to give in and feed off the energy that served me well from within in.

Where the end result had me face another case. It gave me a second chance to belt the corrupt in advance. It was part of a brave test a given opportunity to progress hit the corrupt and follow up on another conquest. I had to trade up and take the trend to the next level.

It had me on the other end bending backward while I give in and pretend. For every trend started again. It was part of a pointless affair that had me face another case feeding off the energy that remained true it gave me a second chance to repeat repel and follow up on another spell.

It had me on the edge forced to pledge, when all become clear al I could sense was a trace that created a piece and forced me off thew edge so I can claim another division to the game. For the drama had given me the energy to feed off the spade, had me forced to erase.

That case that caused an effect broke the silence. So, when I reached my peak, I could return and cover up another sin, just so they can and win another inning. So, when I give in, I fight back and feed off the challenge that had me face that trace. A warning had me waiting to see what will come.

For that challenge had forced me to praise those who entertain me with the notion and the vision. Handing them a proposition. It was part of a trade that had me on the edge, forsaken for another pledge. It was trending for another pause and effect; that broke the silence in the end.

I was way off, trying to claim a division to the game. It was the only way I could resurrect and get back on track and finalise that position that had me waiting for the curse to reverse. I had to follow up on a case to catch and face a hard on. It was part of a mission that had me facing a trial an error.

A terrible tourist, terrorist attack, became visible from the ground up. It became apparent to me that I hit a final degree. It had me on the edge covering up a pledge. Where the corrupt had me warned, left to scheme in-between. Where the lie, become true, energised with force hit back with a rut.

An endorsement, had become apparent and I was hit with a curse that served me well. It had me referred preparing myself for a hurdle. Before I was put through hell. Refusing the corrupt entrance and leading them through the same channel as mine. The difference is, they end up; in a dead end.

I had several hitting a hold up, forced me to reveal and face another case. It caused an effect and presented me with a defect. Pointing it towards a direction that had me face a resurrection. I was on the edge reaping a reward, finalising the impact, preparing me for an encore.

I get in state a fact, feed off the concept. All by entertaining a trace and creating a destination that had me forthcoming. It was forming another investigation. Forced to hit back with remorse where the energy that created the piece forced me release and then without a restriction created peace.

The only trace that served me at the end; was haste. It hit me when I went through that trace. It was part of a trial, that handed me an error. A terrible terror attack that ended in tragedy. It forced me to repeat replay and follow up on one more damn day.

For the game that taught me well forced me through hell. A terrible terror attack brock the silence. It branded me the wrong name and handed the corrupt a brand-new trend. A game that served me well in the end. It gave me a second chance to hit the corrupt in advance.

I was left to give in feed off the win, creating a trace so I can catch up and follow up on another trend. An entrance so I can catch up and face another trend; at the end of the race. It was part of a feast that had me release. It was a trend that had me face another trial in the end.

It caused an effect. It gave me a second chance to get in and feed off the win. Where the corrupt trade up and the tricks to give up and I follow up on another trend. It presented me with a final competition. So, when the time come, I could overcome and free admission.

It had me trapped in the middle of a competition. It had me rephrasing a deception to the corrupts mission. In the long run. It was part of a reason to hit back and feed off the invasion that served me a given. When I hit the end of that invitation it served me a common denomination.

A competition to that mission served me a praise. Just so I can catch up and feed off the sanctity, of that trial and error. It was past remainder of that trend that hit me well in the end. For what I thought was last that resort, was well worth the wait. Every concept had a faith less likely to release.

It caused an effect and took me on a path where every trace became part of a case. An effect that had me resurrect, finalising the trend that saw me break the silence in the end. I had to repeat praise that case feed off the energy that forced its way in; fading away so I can win.

For this time around I was not going to delete nor delay another feat. I had to fade into the distance and face another case, conditioning the mission so I can replace another competition. I had to find peace at the end of that lease. Repeat another revision to that competition.

Where every final repetition, had come and gone and every trial and damn error forced me to hit back with a tremor. It was part a second trial where I get in and feed off the corrupt from within. A trick at the end of that release that had me forced me to hit back with remorse.

It was given a reminder hit in the end of that trend. For that one thing that brought me peace, also gave me the power to undo and devour from within. For the corrupts final manifesto, was the beginning of my declaration of independence. A pure feast, an arrival; towards a survival technique.

The door remained ajar, so I can enter, break the rules, and pretend it never mattered. Still on the run, forced to hit back with a final outcome. I had to feed off the trace that had me erase the case. Try my best to feed off the trace that forced me to replace the case.

The concept became part of a foundation, to follow up on a manifestation. The freedom to help ease the emotional pain, deteriorated; it had me emotionally drained. I had to follow up on a new skill, repeat, and praise those who hit me and ran and fed of me in the long term.

A terminal effect, handing me the trace to end that trend. It forced me to pretend; press delete delay; find my precious way out of that guilt trip. Then pick up where I left off, feed off that tremor handing me a trace that served me a resolution. An institution at the end of that vision.

I had to revive another dive, into that mission that faced me at every competition. It got me through the rough, the tuff and the end of that trend that forced me to override another trace. It was part of a trauma that had me feed of the energy that served me an honour.

I had to work towards the other side where the corrupt returned to repeat another trace; at the end of the race. It had me bake in the cloud; handing me a dead end. An outcome that will put the corrupt through hell. Leaving them suffering in silence. So, I can undo what they did to cover up.

For they entered my realm, covered up the bid. A scheme that served me well in-between. Where I was caught up in a tremor stirring, the pot. They were leading the pact and waiting for the corrupt so I can get back on track. It was part of another trend in the end, all while I create a trace.

It had it had me face another trend in the end. If only they could refresh what they created from that request. Then I would be back where I started feeding off the trend, that handed me a challenge. What a joke I had to evoke, just to catch up. Finalise the trace; at the end of the race.

CHAPTER 5

◆ ◆ ◆

IF ONLY I KNEW WHEN; WHAT WOULD I HAVE DONE NOW?

I was put in a position where I was devalued, left to release that beast. It had me forfeit, a lead; that had me state a fact and break the silence. All so I can carry on to the next pleasure to that lead. I was taught a lesson, given a trace. It had me finalise that treatment, I was lied to; left to refine.

I was given a reason to hit back then follow up on another time. Because there was a tribe in the mist hired to hit run and follow up on an outcome; a given trace. Where I get in repeat rebel and follow up on another trend in the end. Haunting me with a gift, that would not stop giving.

When I hit the end of that trend I was returning for another yearning. Hitting a hold adding to that fold up, with the intention I returned for one more redemption. Then when the time come decline, feed off the trace that had me face another case. It had me facing another cause an effect.

I was feeding of the trend, that had me refine another dead-end. All while I was given a chance to hit back in advance. A release to that feast that forced me to overcome another outcome. Where every release brought out the beast and every foundation gave me the trend to hand me the outcome.

I needed a trend that served me well in the end. It had me pass another dead-end. Where the deception turned into a redemption. It gave me the follow up to return and uncover another trace to that case that caused an effect and presented with an invasion to release temptation.

I fell into a lead, that caused an effect. It brought me an allegation, that had me face an investigation. I had to trade up, give in, and feed off that trap, that had me follow up on a trend. Served well at the end of that allegation. Handing me the confirmation, I need to refine a reification.

For that task, created a dead end. For they decided that every trace had a foundation to repeat another manifestation. For I was led to believe every momentum handed me a clue. It gave me the energy I needed to replace the old and start new. For I was in the middle of a mediation.

Every disturbance handed me a clue; I could not state a fact; nor even get back on track. unless I forced my way in and pretended every trace caused an effect. It gave me the energy to resurrect. I had to face a trace follow up on a feast face a fear. Just to get back on track and finalise the impact.

I was tested with a taste of a vendetta that handed me a clue. The corrupt were so busy praising one another, they forgot I was part of the system that created the piece. I was the one that had come to be and the one that forced my way in; breaking the silence so I can win.

For the faith that handed me a clue was renewed. It forced me to return escape and belt the corrupt right through. I was left to chance and had me embrace a trial and an error. I went as far as blowing a Baritone horn to warn those who think they had power in numbers to hit me and run.

Where they assume they could cause a dilemma, in the long run. Feeding off me as if I was their interpreter. If I did not play it their way I would be there enemy. I owed them my life and they were handing me drama every time the trace became part of a case that had me revered.

I was disrespected by those who knew and fighting back would end worse than the review. I had to return and feed off the trace that had me back on track. I was left to return rebuild feed off the concept and trace those who honour and follow up on a key.

For every time I hit a trend the energy will override, and I start again. While the others were finding an easy way out, targeting me every time they served me doubt. Preparing me for trace that had me face a case. It caused an effect and gave me a presentation that served me a validation.

I was on the move, about to cancel a vendetta. Only to witness the corrupt were staring me at me from another angle. Waiting for me to fail, because they made me weak and frail, just so they can prevail. Assuming preventing from entering the Holy Grail will hand them hope.

I then lose, trapped in the middle of a competition it had me stepping into a proposal that served me a trace that had me face another trial and error. It was to hand me admission force me to hit back with a competition. A trace that will treat me like a victim, harming me at every disposal.

Where the outcome, becomes part of a track record, where I get in and prepare myself for another win. I no longer end up dead at the end of the race. For the method now has become my way of letting go. Not only I survive but I am alive and I am returning to hump those who harmed me.

Preventing the corrupt from ever entering. Because I had to embrace another case, where the key became informative. I ended up stepping into the unknown, creating a challenge that had me out grow and undo a follow up. Repeating a review; straight in to the next common clue.

Opening an investigation, was the only way for me to prepare myself. Because I was led on taught a lesson, left to repeat. Where the only challenge I had was the one that took me in and failed me from within. Where the corrupts method become benevolent, just for my entertainment.

I faced my fear, took control of the key and the corrupts finally. Leaving no trail behind, no trace to embrace, no dignity to erase either. Because their survival technique had arrived to early, I got in. Hitting the corrupt from within; waiting for that conspiracy to end.

I survived to tell the story of who when and where it all begun, where every challenge saw me as a gift a trace that hit me at the end of the race. I could not help to think it was a plot to push me off the edge; straight into a ditch. Just so the corrupt can return for another pitch.

Continue on their journey holding me hostage. Holding a grudge, assuming I agreed to their terms and conditions. Just to see the end, come to be; following up on another premonition. Just to follow up on anther survival, to that trace that handed me a key; a brand-new grand entrance.

Because I fell into a heap, it broke the silence. Torn in between two worlds; the old and the new. A freeride, for the corrupt to franchise. A challenge I never knew, had come and gone. It tested my patience and repeated, until I was forced off the edge straight into a journey.

It led me towards a path that had me rise up and feed off the trend. It served the corrupt an ending that was handing me the insurance. I was given an opportunity to invade in the privacy of those who invaded in mine. Making sure they never rise above and beyond that declaration.

A decision to accommodate that restoration to that manifestation. Had come and gone, it handed me a clue and prevented me from overriding another review. It handed me on the road to recovery a chance to interact with a trace that had me overlap with a vision; serving me a competition.

An informal investigation, from that interaction, caused an effect. It faced me with a debt; it trapped me in the corner and gave me a chance to embrace another trace. When I hit the end of the race the energy that caused an effect handed me the evaluation; just to trick the corrupt at every destination

A concept that threw me off the edge. Straight into Humble beginnings and unprecedented endings. Prepared me for a case, that had me face another trace. It had me return, replace a new trend in the end. For they forced me of the edge straight into a narrative where I became negative.

Where I should be positive, but I lost my way, my light dimmed the freedom I once had; was taken away from me. The only thing was the drama and the trend that led me towards a journey that had me forced to pretend. It caused an effect and broke the corrupts silence all so I can catch up.

I was off with the fairies, trying make sense of my hardship. I was handed a key; it forced me to release that beast. I was in demand, several wanted my key, only to witness that key was a challenge that will stuff them all have them suffer in sin while I catch up and feed off that win.

It was pointless affair that handed me the breach, to break the silence. I was hit with violence while fast forwarding to the next step belting the corrupt so I never resurrect. It was handing me a final leaving the corrupt living in denial. It had me sail through, with several turbulent challenges.

I was long overdue, a long way away; trying to get through. I had to remain afloat from that journey that pushed me off the edge. I was hitting a curse, I could not reverse, nor rehearse because I fell in a trap. It had me heaving getting back on track forming a burst of energy to release that tension.

It was tormenting me every waking moment. I had to let go and face my fear; all in one setting. I had to heave at every trace, give in, and repeat while the rest compete. I had the corrupt belt me from within. It had me giving in letting them come first so they win and feed off me from within

It had me in admin living a lie, waiting to be called up and break the silence from within to get by. It was giving me a vibe, to stay alive, a spurt of energy, enough to release that demon to erase that corruption that had me reliving a night mare in my disposition to that desperation.

I was to harm the corrupt at every evaluation, a mission was put on hold the competition. It was stating a fact and the key to the next threat. It became part of a debt that forced me to release that forthcoming event. It had me push the corrupt in the corner so I can vent.

I had to find peace and raid the heads of he who hit me and ran. Projecting those keys, towards the next case. An informative event that had me erase that case causing an effect, preventing the corrupt from returning for a yearning. The competition had me experienced; wasting away no more.

I had failed a vision, one hell of a competition. Not only I was put in a position where I was let down forced to praise, he who kidnapped me to stay alive. But those who knew returned to belt me to the ground. It had me stepping into the unknown warned once again feeding off the dead end.

I was failing again, handed a trap that served me a case that led me to believe that edge had no freedom to revive another technique. Because I was too busy trying to release and find peace a follow up to that piece come to be facing me with a new reality.

I had to return, repeat, giving into those who delete. Delaying a follow up on a play; a trip down memory lane. Stirring the pot every single step of the way. Time flew and I kept missing the boat I had to repeat follow up on a new. So, when the time, come the only thing left was the outcome.

I had to release that beast, I was return and test the patience of those who retaliated. So, when I hit the end of that trend it had me facing another dead end. When those who got in before I; were to support me; when I reached. But they turned against me, they broke the chain handing me a cane.

The contract was breached, they started a fight, rounding it up to a new contract. It had me cornered because they rounded up the troops. Tricked into thinking otherwise, so when I reached my peak my second trail would be deleted. Where the only thing left was the presentation.

They handed me an evaluation that failed me periodically. I was left torn; mistaken for a fool. So, when I reached my peak, it will turn against those who restored their energy by harming me periodically. It was presenting me with a trace and a taste of a filthy dirty trick.

A presentation that had me risk my dream, forcing me to return and redeem. Breaking the corrupts spirit in-between. The cycle of events was tangled in a web of lies. I was left stranded struggling to get back on track, feeding off a contest. It had me reach my peak handing me a hat trick.

It had forced the corrupt to repeat another trace. Where this time around I actually hear the truth. Breaking that trends leading them all to a dead end. Where I get in and target them all from within. Where getting by will be a task that will help me overcome; another dead-end in the long run.

I felt strangled, by the whole ordeal. It handed me a violation to that jurisdiction. Where the corrupt saw the vision stole my key and left me haunted by the past. Living in the present waiting for the corrupt to fail so I can prevail. Warning me that every test was part of a request.

It had me warned, I had to retaliate by hitting them with same game; handing them the cane. While I get back on track and gush with; liquidation to that manifestation. I had to rise above that trend belting the corrupt once again. Poisoned by the break that handed me; love then hate.

Leaving me disheartened by the past, wanting to return for a vendetta. Every time I hit back, the trace, pushed me off track and forced me to repeat. It had me leaving the corrupt returning to release that feast. I had to press delete delay and follow up on a brand-new game; to that bad day.

It forced me off the edge straight into an expense, that had me retaliating at the end of that trend. It forced me to pretend; just to find peace, about to face another case. Repeating an unnecessary test. An urge served me a curse at the end of that verse; cheated at every level.

Breaking the rules and leaving me feeding off the end. It was handing the corrupt a dead-end. They were to steal my key and my identity. It was pushing me off the edge, trapped in the middle of a debt, and a dead-end reality. I was threatened by the whole concept torn at every final.

I was being judged, left to suffer in silence; about to end up in an asylum. In hindsight I was sorted out, put in a position where I knew no doubt. I lived my life, lit a flame fell into a trace, and broke the silence all the same. Assuming that was it, I was about to hit; in fact, it was beginning of a new hint.

I was lied to, traced tricked forced to release a new feast. Warned that the atmosphere that followed, changed and the power to project was rearranged. It had me face another case conditioning the mission repeating another competition; with the same concept.

So, when all else failed, I could enter that realm with the outlook of knowing. I hit the end of that trend. Preventing the corrupt from re-entering and starting again. It was part of a feed, that served me well; creating a new breed. Put through hell trapped in the middle of a spell.

I had to remain silent give in and feed off the entrance that failed me at the end of that trace that had me face another case from within. I was way off trying to put together another missing piece to a puzzle that had me release another test; on request. Find peace, in the end of that feast.

But all it did was have me engage in another rage. Finalising that ending that had me pending. Causing an effect and preparing for another defect. For those who entered my realm unworthy hit me with a trace that was pending. It forced me to pretend and follow up on another trend.

An alarming momentum, forced me to hit back with a spectrum. It became part of a huge warning; it had me facing another yearning. For what was to come from that outcome, had me step into the unknown. Facing a creativity, about to burn into flames; then glorify the yearning in-between.

It was part of a trace, at the end of the race. Forcing me to replace that case. Waiting for me to fail so the corrupt can replace me with another hit. In fact, replacing me now was no longer part of the mission. I made my mark; I created the piece waited for the corrupt to pay me out; from that feast.

I was stepping into the unknown, breaking the silence; that remained sweet. It was leading me towards a destination, forcing me to release that demon. It had me warned of what was to come from that outcome. Thet were causing an effect a tendency to reach above with a regret.

It was beyond repair; there were to many hang ups. Where I thought, I was lied to, laughed at left to remain silent, all while the corrupt hit me with a gamble at the end of that sample. A simple way to expressing my gratitude and follow up to the next final review.

It was a journey long overdue too long to renew. Even though I concluded it with a warning. I hit a resolution, revolutionising that constitution. I could not reveal more than I could chew. But I could move on and feed off that track that served me wrong.

It was leading me to a dead end, no resurrection. The trace was too hard to replace; it was way too easy; to repeat. Gone were the days, where the corrupt were to hit me and run. Trying to harm and end my flight for nothing. They were mistaken for a forsaken role; a journey that fed off me whole.

CHAPTER 6

WHEN THE CORRUPT COVER UP RETURNING THE FAVOUR

The test had become part of a trace, that had been pending. I was led on, left to believe that the trend was passed on. I was part of a test that was too hard to embrace. Where the easy part became part of a trend that had been pending landing me in a role handing me a dead end.

I had to compel against the will of those who thought entering my realm will hand them forethought. I was to combine, whatever come my way, for every trace was based on a case that was pending. It had me resurrect finalise that test; that had me aligned with a request.

An entitlement at the end of the race, had become presentable. I hit an inevitable response to that trial, that created an erratic thought. It had me belting the corrupt at the last resort. I had to unravel a scheme, undo a theme, try my luck creating a trend in the end.

It had me feed off a trial an error an end to that terror. It had me encouraging the corrupt, to repeat and rebel against one another. All so I can finalise that trend and feed off the tremor, that hit in the end. It had me facing another enigma while I go through hell.

Where every trace and every journey had me embrace another case. All because every journey I was on, remained strong. I was aligned with a trend, that faced me with a verse, I could reverse; in the end. It had me wasting another damn day, repeating what I thought was part of a method.

I had to remain strong, because every trace had me face another uncanny case. I had to throw the old, and create a new trace. Stir the pot and follow up on another trend, just to get back on track and pretend. It was part of an unbiased prediction that led me towards the next jurisdiction.

Given a final reveal, reviving on what I thought was part of a steal a trace that had me undoing a case. It was handing me the indication; I hit a hold up. It pushed me off track, took me on a journey that had me facing the facts. In fact, it was part of a trend, that had me pending for a dead end.

A curse I could not reverse; it was rehearsed. It had come and gone; and left a mark. It forced its way in, lining me up for another win. I was on my path hitting an ending to that stream; veering towards the wrong direction. For every curse created a manoeuvre, to help the corrupt outdo a review.

I had to overcome and screw those who knew, just to point the finger at he who had a clue. For those who did not think it through, got through. They had done no more damage than those who assumed. Where hitting and running, will be the end of that forthcoming.

Because hitting me and running, had served me a wrong doing. I was stuck on the path of wrapping up the old starting new and breaking the silence of he who knew and he who had a clue. For a while there was a free ride, to override the old the new and the trace that took me in.

Taken for a fool, fed off from within, waiting for the right moment to repeat. I had to reclaim my vision break that cycle that hit me at every proposition. It was harming my every being, troubling me at every scent. Where the drama took over my well-being, and the only thing left was the trend.

A trace that was pending in the end, became evident. I was taught a lesson left to disregard the corrupt. Just so I can return, finalise that feast that served me well. It broke me when I hit the end of that spell. In fact, I was harming my self-trying to get through; fighting with that demon who knew.

That one demon who became, attached to my spirit; caused an effect. It took me on a journey that served me well. Then when the pot was hot let me go; no longer following up on a new show. For the corrupt had me mortified, beyond disbelief. I was taught a lesson and left to rummage through.

It was part of a trace that caused an effect. Where every curtain closed and every faith took a wrong turn. I was left open to discussion; I had to repeat retaliate and press delete. Delaying every concept removing every clue; hitting an ending that was pending. A trap, that was damaging my every move.

I was put on hold, held captive; captivated by the holy spirit. I to was put through worse, than he who knew. For he who had a clue saw me as an easy target, trying to confide and follow up on a dive. I was put in a position that had me face a trace causing an effect a presentation that seized.

Where the Corporate affairs took a faith less likely to compete. I had to trace; embrace take the initiative and feed off the trend. It forced me off the bend, a challenge that had me step into the unknown, heaving at me every time I was handed a clean way out.

Every trace had a trend, where every follow up, took me on a final journey. I could no longer pretend because I was too busy fighting off the demon. The one that remained on my raider watching me like A hawk waiting for me to fail so they can prevail. It was belting me trying to break my spirit.

I had to return exchange, rearrange, and follow up on another trace. It had me pretending, I was on the mend. Waiting patiently for the corrupt to overcome; all, so I can underestimate the outcome. Because I took it as a fault it had me hit the remote. I had to pause an effect and create an entrance.

I was meant to enter, feel free, and uncover up another unprecedented key. For the corrupt were to fail and never resurrect, because I was found easy, trapped in the middle of an ordeal. Where the end had me face another trace. It was forcing me to return and surplus another trend in the end.

It was finalising that presentation, handing me the confirmation I needed to break the silence. It had me feed off the trial the error and the final vendetta. A feast, that served me a lineup, that broke the system. It forced me to reject another competition. Before I was hit with a challenge that seized.

I was to endeavour to never say never, get back on track; feeding off that vendetta. The one thing that had me facing another violation to that manifestation. In the end of that trailer, it became part of a trace, that had me on the edge failing every case. Truly I was hitting a dead-end; to that summit.

I had no reason to replace that treason, it was part of an extension. It brought me forward, a tension to that redemption. It became part of a restitution, to the corrupts communion. I was on the lookout for a key, to fix my anxiety. Only to witness I hit a final degree, a task that lost its thrust.

Handing me a test that had me request a confirmation. It had me stepping in to a trace validating what I knew to be true. It served me well at the end of that spell. I was taught a lesson, where I had to relive another confirmation to that everlasting key.

Served a faith, less likely to return; just feed off the burn. It gave me the power to rely no one but my spirit to get by. It was handing the corrupt a test that forced me to refresh then cover up another trace to that mass; confirming the obvious. For the corrupt lost its skill and collapsed remaining still.

The trace becomes part of a trend, where every motivation took me on a path; where I was relisted. I fell into wrath a senseless taste of reality to embrace. So, every trend will kick in, handing me the resolution I needed to break free from that external feast that broke my spirit in the end.

For that trend warned me in the end I had nowhere to turn but back to the enemy to finalise that feast that harmed me at the end of that piece. Where every preservation had me forming an investigation releasing what I thought was the end of that trend that forced me to pretend.

I had to face a fact, challenge the method that had me measure what I thought was the last resort. It gave me a second chance to break the cycle in advance. So, when I hit the end of that road the trace became remorseful, the treasure hunt extensive. it caused an effect and forced me to resurrect.

It forced the corrupt to repeat and rebel against the trace that had me follow up on another vision. It had me on the edge, competing and compelling against an entrance. It served me a competition to give in to that test. The method had become a conquest. I was tracked down, forced to repeat.

Just to get back on track. Where every trace had me forced to replace and follow up on another case. It was to give in and finalise that method from within. For that piece that had me release, cause and effect, tracked me down and led me towards a journey that had me face another case.

It was trapping he who could replace, that trace. A journey that caused and effect and created a foundation that forced me to hit back with another manifestation. I could not erase, or keep up with the program. For each case, had its own review, it caused an effect and created a defect.

I was presented with a false alarm; it was breaking the silence. It had me race up and down trying to find peace, from that trauma. I was left hitting a dead end facing another traumatic effect. Only to find that is what was keeping me alive. Handing me a challenge that served me well.

It presented me with an ongoing test, that faced me with a presentation that handed me an allegation. I was on the edge, where every trace saw me as an easy target.

Restored my energy and forced me to hit back with a violation; to that manifestation. An ending to that request.

I was on the edge, feeding of the trend; that served me well in the end. It had me resurrect finalising each faith presenting me with a chaotic event. It had me reach my pinnacle and prevent the corrupt from holding on to another symmetry. Where I was given a reason to hit back with treason.

A failed attempt, that was causing the wrong effects, became evident. It was leading the wrong, down a path to harm. Where those who were on their road, were to overcoming another task. I had to recover every trace, trying my luck by feeding off the burn that forced me to return.

It was breaking the silence that had me face another trace, it had me step into the unknown. I was forced to hit back with remorse. I was taught a lesson left to repeat another competition so when I hit that task. Where the only fresh thing left was the energy that forced me to hit back with regret.

A trend that led me towards a journey that had me breaking the cycle; in the end. A trend where, there was no freedom nor foundation to pretend. Just an evaluation to restore my energy and start again. I was stuck trying to get out of a threat. Where a simple task, dragged on, for way too long.

I was left hitting the end of that wrath, I was forcing myself to stop. I had to think things through and every time I thought I was stuck in the same game; stuck in a rut. It was hitting an ending that was pending and a trace that was somewhat never ending. A challenge that was harming my spirit.

I was on the path of returning for a yearning. It was creating a piece that will restore my energy and follow up on another feast. I had to return and repeat, for what I thought was the last resort was the beginning of an end. I had to return and create a trace that had me replace another case.

I was on the path of facing a trend, it had me forcing myself to create a new improved dead end. The truth had set me set me. I was led to release follow up on another feast. I had to catch the corrupt at every feast. Restoring my energy so I can find peace; waiting for the concept to come to an end.

It had me finalise that trace, it took me on a journey that forced me to repeat. I had to replace a follow up on a trend to back myself up in the end. It had me set free, conditioning the mission so I can return and establish a competition. For he who created the piece forced me to release.

I was trying my luck to finalise that feast in the end of that trace. It had me replace a case; heaving at me at every place. For he who caused an effect had me follow up another threat, it was restoring my energy and creating a foundation that had me repeating another confirmation.

In the end, I was torn left to hit back, face another fact

and feed off the trace. Just to get back on track, only to witness the only thing left was to let go and follow up on a journey that will hand me the power to outdo undergo a follow up on another show grounding hew who knew.

I was facing another trend it had me face a dead end. For what I thought was the last resort had me face another trace feed off the edge that had me hit the end of that foundation. It forced me to pledge. It gave me a chance to override that subsidy that handed me the energy to feed off the end.

I had to trace undo the case and finalise the entrance that faced me with a vengeance. As if I did not know what was about to occur. So, I had to return hit back with a vengeance a chance to break the corrupts cycle of events. A trace leading them towards a journey where they cannot replace.

Because I was given the freedom to hit back with treason, it handed me a passion. Where the corrupt were handing me poison and every journey I was on had me facing another long road. Towards a path that served me a raise to that praise. It had facing me a curse at every verse.

Where I had to let go, reward myself and undo what I thought was the last resort. In fact, it was the beginning of a new clue, in the end. I was forced to repeat return for one more chance to create a trace and belt the corrupt in advance. All while I reveal the corrupts motive to that screen of themes.

It was my way to catch up feed off the drama, I was traumatised, led to believe that every cause an effect created a piece and forced me to undo and release peace. It was part of an action that presented me with an abreaction. It caused an effect that served me wrong.

I was pushed me in the corner; causing havoc all while I remained strong. It handed me an enigma, that faced me, at the end of that trend. It had me question every motivation even taking me for a ride to the next destination. It was presenting me with a final investigation.

I was surrounded by several, who had me cornered, feeding off the trace that failed me at the end of the race. It took me on a journey, that led me towards a presentation, that broke the system. It had my foundation cracked in several forms. Where I had to return and hit back with undertaking.

It caused an effect and created a piece; it led me towards a destination, where I get in. Feed off the trace trapo those who comply then delete delay and push the corrupt in the corner just before I get in and press replay. It served well from within ending the race and handing the corrupt a final trace.

Where in the end the race rewarded me with a case. It was part of a validation violating every move and feeding off the trend that served me well in the end. I was hit with a kind heart, a challenge where every time I was served a trace, the ending will give in and hand me a brand-new case.

The corrupt had me forced to hit back at every disposal. It had on the edge preaching their knowledge, assuming I gave a damn. In fact, I was reliving a nightmare and surviving on truth. I had to smooth the groove, trap the trace, and trick and track the corrupt down at the end of the race.

Belting the corrupts method whenever I saw fit it. It had me feed off the concept, create a piece follow up on a feat. Trap he who knew and make sure he who had a clue; lose hindsight of the truth. I was being forced to hit back with an encore. I had to feed off the trauma, and hit at every disposal.

I was taught a lesson, rejecting a recommendation because it was false fake and misleading. All so I can reclaim another deception to that mission. It was warning me I hit a final release it had me facing another trace; that was pending. It had me release that feast forced to hit back with remorse.

I was returning for a feast, trapped in the middle of a release. The energy that created the piece, had me return for a favour, all so I can find peace. I had to find a way to retaliate and release that redemption that had me facing another trend in the end of that tactful momentum.

It forced me to restart and break the silence; it had me face a trace. A dead to that mission that lined me up for a competition. All while I hit the end of that treasure that forced me to release that beast. It took me in and faced me with a challenge. A new beginning, a fresh start; a win to that inning.

I was trapped in the middle of a stagnant affair. All while the corrupt took me for a fool. Then attempted to feed off the method, warning me there was no faith to that rule. I had no trace, and the trick became a challenge to invade in that rule that had me remain silent too.

I had to follow up on an entrance, to that trend. Presented me with a dead end. I had to embrace. give in, trap that trend and create an extension to that redemption. All so I can cave in on the concept skip that feast and fail the corrupts method so I can find peace.

CHAPTER 7

◆◆◆

WHEN THE CORRUPT GET CAUGHT WITH EMBEZZELMENT!

I was on the mission, trying to come to terms with the fact, I was caught up in a trace. It had me fast forwarding to the next competition. I had a pending gift, where I had to carry it to the next level. The only way through was to undo a past event. It served me well and presented me with a key.

It was a never ending, challenge that forced me to review and keep up with the program. It was for me to catch up feed off the corrupt and follow up on another skill. It had me face another trace causing an effect and helping me get back on track; breaking the cycle from within.

I had failed one test; it created a trend that served me well in the end. Forced through hell, it led me to believe every trace had me facing a trend; at the end of the race. Those who knew and those who had a clue were fooled. Giving me a chance to unfold plant a seed; creating a follow up in-between.

It had me facing another case, giving into those who challenged me. I had to undo and face another final degree. It had me trying to case every trace, that had me forced to repeat and rebel against those who serve me well. It was testing the patience of those who cut and paste.

It had me in control returning the favour so I can pledge. It had me sitting on an angle, forced to repeat and rebel against those who put me through hell. I was on the edge, of reason, trapped in the middle of a trend that served me well in the end. I had been forced to hit back with a need.

A dirty trick, that had me repeat, started a journey that had me face another trace. I was hitting the corrupt at the end of the race. I had to report, get back on track, and follow up on a treatment that led me to believe that every case had me on the run; ready to replace a wild attack.

Hand that attack back to the sender threefold. Just so I can catch up cause an effect create a war in the corrupts defect. I had to finalise the truth face another case feed off the system and replace it with a curse I can reverse and finalise the system handing the corrupt a brand-new vision.

Just before I was handed an encore, the journey that served me was uncanny. I was taught a lesson left to repeat at every momentum. I was given a chance to hit back in advance, where the trace was pardoned. I was trapped, tricked, and taken for a ride; just to erase another case.

A chance to dive into a method that forced me to replace a case. It warned me I was on the edge; trapped me in the middle of that riddle. It had me face a condition towards a mission that served me well at every presentation. Returning for one more competition, just to cast a spell.

It was hitting the corrupt at every turn, just to get a glimpse of a trace that had me replace a case. I to undo that method that forced me to review and follow up on another trend in the end. It had me foreclose a trip down memory lane. A given reason to repeat and reclaim another competition.

It was part of the corrupts method. Where I had to face a truth, terrorise and justify those who use me to recline and reclaim another division to the game. For that path I was on, was part of a reality check. I had to feed off the corrupt at every mortality hitting back with morality.

It had me challenge that stagnant affair, it served me well; at every forthcoming spell. Pretending there was a trend that was never-ending. It was part of a past case, that caused an effect. It led me towards a presentation that forced me to repeat a challenge.

Where the corrupts method, had me face another trace. All so I can press delete, delay, and present the corrupt with foreplay. A path that had me reserve the right to accommodate another. It gave me a chance to force my way in and feed off the corruption; that was about to feed off me.

It was part of a trap, to hand me an ordeal. I was led to believe that the energy I was creating was stagnating. In fact, it was causing an effect pausing every trend, it had me on the edge wrapped in silence hitting a trend that become part of that return that red between the lines.

It was handing me an evaluation to break the silence. I was to hit the corrupt with a vengeance. It had me step forward following up on a feast. An incantation to repeat an interrogation. Violating the truth and forcing myself to align that stagnation; handing me a brand-new investigation.

The key I needed to break the silence; forced its way in. It fed off the drama that served me well from within. For those who were in, had me facing a trace to that case. It was causing an effect, assuming that it will engrave their name to the game. It had me facing a trace, that played its part.

It was presenting me with a dead end in the end. It gave me a chance to delve into a trace, where that challenge returned with a vengeance. It was handing me the energy to violate the system. Where the corrupts method will break the cycle right into an extreme theme.

While I end up wild in nature, safe and pure; a Devine Defender of mankind. Where I get in play my role and resurrect feeding of the corrupt whole. Finalise that trend that had me facing a dead end. It was pointing its trace towards a journey that led me through hell.

It was presenting me with a journey that remained strong. It kept me waiting long enough to see I was being used in a sorority created by the minority. It fed off me from within breaking my wing. I was once again replaced me with an absolute dud. It had no energy nor creativity to praise apiece.

The chance I was handed was branded. I went through it all, and hit a final review. I went in heaved at that trend that warned me in the end there was no faith less likely to pretend. For hell froze over and that is when I knew I hit a demon. Who had no freedom; because he worked for the system.

I worked solo and my system had reached its peak. I was forced to renter and face another trace just to get in and feed off the drama from within. I had to face another trace to that case that caused an effect. For every momentum broke the system and silence was restored.

The rules were changed, the challenge rearranged. Every time I reached my peak, I was forced to repeat. I had to rebel, return, then report those who put me through hell. For every test had its momentum and I had hit my peak, rise up, praise, break the silence; serve me a brand-new phase.

For every trace had me on the mend, pausing an effect. It had me trapping those who resurrect. I had to return, let them in, and then restrict them from re-entering and harming me again. It was an entertaining event; I was left to break the trend. A trace that nevertheless ended with a force.

Unless I caused an effect and surrendered the trace. The presentation would have caused an effect and handed me the entertainment. Where I needed to restore my energy and resurrect. It was to override and undertake another trace to that case. A given challenge that handed me a key.

It gave me a second chance to belt the corrupt in advance. It was part of a test that forced me to progress. It gave me a presentation that served me well at every final investigation. I was taught a lesson warning the corrupt that the trend was based on a compelling comprehension.

It had me on the mend, trapping those who pretend. It gave me a second chance to hit back in advance. I was left trapped in a trend that had me break the cycle in the end. I was taught a lesson left to repeat; it gave me a second chance to press delete. All while I delay forced to hit the corrupt.

I was taught a lesson left to repeat. It handed me an emotional trauma; so, I can press delete. It trapped me and handed me a clue; it caused an effect and troubled me in the end. All so I can resurrect and face the corrupt;

paying off a debt. It had me process at the end of that final bend.

It had me press delete, just before I hit an encore. It gave me a second chance to release that beast. I was forced to find peace after the fact. All so I give in and prevent the corrupt from releasing another demon from within. So, when I caught up, I could release and follow up on another trace.

I had to follow through undo another review. It had me face another trace that presented me with a final testimony that case that had me erase what I thought was the last resort. It served me well and presented me with an upcoming spell. I had to refine and hit back while the rest decline.

All so, I can cave in on the concept and create a trend that will hand me a dead end. What I had to do was just to find peace in the end. Where in the end of that second trial, it handed me denial. It was uncanny, I was left to erase, embrace and give in to that fall that served me well from within.

All while the corrupt invade in what I call a recall. I was presented with a gift hit back with a cause, then when the time come overcome another outcome. For the corrupt, had me facing a trace hitting a trend breaking the silence and starting again. A trend that had me face another dead-end.

All while I was causing an effect, trapped in the middle of a defect. Harming those who get by, assuming those who knew were about to get in and finalise that deception from within. For all I knew I had no freedom to skip that too. For I was given a chance to release that beast.

It presented the corrupt with another feast. I was given an expense that served me well; at the end of that trend. It was the way out for me. It put the corrupt through hell all the way. It gave me a second chance to return and press repay. Just to hand the corrupt a dead end; all the way.

It had me force to hit back with remorse. I was cancelled out, even before I had a chance to repeat it. It became less likely for me to outdo another clue; it had me overcome an outcome. Because the corrupt worked in unison. Stepping into the unknown was forcing me to outdo another review.

I had to flourish, let go and feed off the no show, I had a final review. It gave me the power to decline and read between the lines. I had to keep up with the program; with an upkeep. I was to give in, and prepare myself for another trace given the power to hit back and devour.

For those who entered my realm tried their luck, assuming that the trace will hand me bad luck. For the curse had me reverse all while the corrupt rehearse. It was hitting me on a periodic effect. Handing me the conclusion and the trace to return the favour and erase.

For that case caused an effect and repeated, just so I can catch up and finalise that trend that left me pushing forward and facing a dead-end. I was well in trying my hardest to get in. It handed me a resolution to embrace the case and kick up a fuss all while I get back on track and finalise that trend.

I was hit with an ending that had been pending for a while. I was stirring the pot catching base finalising that trend and feeding off the given; all so, I no longer have to pretend. Just to delete delay and follow up on a replay. All while I give in and break the silence from within.

Every trace, had me return and replace; whatever come my way. It gave me a second chance to hit back in advance. Every task messed up my head, waiting patiently to create a trace so I can catch up and feed off the dead end. I was on the move, warned of what was to come from that outcome.

For I was left to pretend, finalise that trend that had me facing another dead-end. I was left to trace and trap that test that was pending it was part of a never-ending battle. A case that had me repair trap and treat the corrupt with utter most disrespect so I can get back on track and resurrect.

I had to lie, to the corrupt so I can trap them. Then take the initiative, wrap them up, forcing the corrupt to outdo he who tried his luck. I had to embrace what I thought was part of the race. It was part of a challenge, that had me stepping into the unknown forcing me to redo and reclaim a review.

I had to fight back then hit back with a structure; to face the corrupt all so I can get back on track. It had me on the edge, facing a debt, just before I had a chance to hit back in advance. I was led on taught a lesson it gave me a chance to break the cycle and create a challenge that will serve me well.

I was forced to hit back with remorse, restoring an energy that had me face another trace. All while I get back on track and feed off the course. It had me face another case trapped in the middle of a coercion by the corrupt so they can return and cover up another hold up.

It served me well when I was forced to treat, trap and challenge the corrupt at thew end of that trend. All so I can feed off the edge repeating a trace, I was returning for a favour and causing an effect. All while I reach my peak and create a trend to help me press delete.

I had to repeat catch base, face up to the consequences to the case while I press delete. Then when the time come overcome an energy, that faced me in the end. It was forcing me to undo and pretend. It had me stepping forward, facing a fact, causing an effect; helping me get back on track.

It led me towards a second trial. I had to face the corrupt, with an endearment; not feed off the tread. I had no kind word no foundation to break the train of thought. Where every trace handed me an evaluation to repeat just to kindly state a fact. All so I can get back on track; break the silence.

The faith that had me raid the head of he who hunted me down. Warned me I hit the energy that took me in. It forced me to replace redo and follow up on another review. I was rewarded with a chance to advance then take the initiative and follow up on a review.

Feeding off the concept so I can skip that too, had me facing another trace so I can claim another division to that game. Where the presentation had elevated and I was delegating to the next. Forcing the corrupt to hit back and resurrect, presenting me with a final review.

I had to catch up break the silence follow up on a faith that had me reach my peak face another daze so I can press delete. It was part of a challenge that will serve me right, it handed me a chance to face another trace repeating what I knew and creating a challenge to help me face and skip that too.

A trend that had me hitting a dead end, served me well. It gave me a chance to face the corrupt in advance. I was on the move about to hit a final reserve, just to recap, what I thought was the last resort. So, when I caught up and forced my way in, I regret my thoughts; where my faith turned.

It was no worse than the hit, faced with a case that had me return for a vendetta. It had me on the edge of trapping those who pledge. It created a trace that took me in and forced me to return for one more key. Because I was stuck in a fantasy where the reality took its toll I lived in a lie.

It was part of a trace where I was imagining an unrealistic truth. Just so I can return and feed off the trauma that forced me to face the facts. It was part of a pointless affair where I was hit with a trend that had me overcome a trap in the end. I had to concluded all where every trace served me a case.

I was belted to the point where I lost my will and the pleasure to hit back with leisure. I had to redo another review. I was turned, returning for another yearning. Where every time I could undo a review, everything became a challenge and nothing was done; because I hit a hold.

It was part of a trace, that served me unwillingly, it created a trend that pushed me out of place. For every time I hit a hold up, I was forced to hit back and skip the corrupt; all so I can get back on track. For every direction had me facing another reception to that resurrection.

Feeding off the resurrection, was part of the deception. The other part was part of a terrible lie, that became part of my path that made me face another trace. It was intriguing, I had to grasp for air, condition the mission face another diversion all while I hit the corrupt with a brand-new mission.

The wait was over; all I knew every time I was left to decline. The journey and the trace were harming me. Leaving me profound, creating a war in those who hit back and face the facts. It was waiting for me to trap those who have the energy to fight back with a conscious awareness.

For they were the ones that led the pact, it was leading them towards a journey that had me facing another trace. Abort to abort and enter preparing me for another treasure. Failing every momentum, creating a stagnation to that manifestation that hit me when I hit the end of that trend.

When I reached that trend the new trace caused an effect; it created a dead end. It taught me a lesson, a chance to return for a trace at the end of the race. Where I was given a reason to hit back with treason. Where I had to overcome and hit back with a trial an error; a long-term effect.

CHAPTER 8

◆◆◆

WHEN SHIT HITS THE FAN & THE CORRUPT CIRCULATE; BACK IN MOTION

I was taught a lesson and the only way out was the way in. Even then; Heaven hit Earth and hell come first. The trace became part of a race, towards a finish line. It had me face another trend in the end, so when the corrupt saw me easy they caved in on me and left me unreasonably unhappy.

There was a challenge, that had me return and follow up on a skill. I was working towards a fascination that handed me the interrogation that forced me to return and break the corrupts spirit. A brand-new foundation that had me on the lookout wanting to release that beast.

A feast that forced me to hit back and release peace. It had me on the edge sitting pretty while the corrupt were forced to hit back with remorse. I had to feed off the trace that had me face another case. Because I took it all in and faced another trap; I was handed a presentation.

It was validating the obvious after the fact, it had me forced to repeat and face a trace. I was handed a clue and hit back with a review. It faced me with a fear, just so I can catch up and present the corrupt with a challenge that had me repeat, replace, and get back on track; feeding off the case.

It had me facing another trend, it broke the silence and faced me with a trial and error in the end. It was causing an effect and feeding off the terror. It had me on the other end, starting again. It handed me a key that served me a trace. It had me replace the old the new; the forthcoming clue.

I had to repeat, follow up on a trace, then trick the corrupt, so I can catch up and finalise that trend that had me fail in the end. I was led on taught a lesson left to repeat rebel against those who force me delete. So, when I give in the only torture was the one that truly left me to feed off the sin.

It was the one thing that had me feed off that quest. It gave me the power to undo and devour. I was on the edge, facing another trace. It was giving me the power to prevent the corrupt from dividing conquering. It was deleting that quest that forced me to undo that review.

I was on a mission, to request a recount and a new test. One that will meet my criteria and prevent me from hitting a challenge that forced me to break the silence and follow up on a review hitting back while I skip that too. It was forcing the corrupt to begin a new win.

I was trapped, into a trend, it had me facing a dead-end. I was pushed in a trace that had me face another case. It caused an effect, brought me forward, leading me to a transformation; that made me hate civilization. I was caught in a faith that weighed me down it had me facing a dead end.

A challenge that took me on a journey, that had me returning for a yearning. I was put in a position walking straight into an oblivion. Just so I can condition the mission and reap a reward. It had me face a violation to that next destination. Where the progress feed off the quest; so, I can digress.

The troubles I faced was part of a case; I was misled misjudged and taken for a fool. It had me sit on a bench, waiting patiently to vent, all while the rest reap a reward and follow up on an energy that forced me to repeat. I was taken away from my family by those who saw my potential.

Assuming stealing my key, will bring them unity. In fact, all it did was create an artifact, a chance for me to build around my truth and my passion. Where I continue to build and face my days, knowing each momentum will bring me peace. It had me finalise that tension so I can release.

It was part of a challenge, that was presenting the corrupt with a final beast. Where I was on the move, trying my luck taking the initiative and replacing that trace that forced me to give in feeding off the win. I was presented with a task that had me relive a nightmare.

It was part of a trace that had me repeat and replace. It was a given momentum, that forced me to redo, restore and follow up on a curse I can reverse. I had to replace and finalise that trend that belted me on a continuous basis. All so I lose my fight, follow up on a feat, and face another treat.

It was part of a violent ending, that had me pending. A trace at the end of that piece, had served me well. It was preparing me for the next entrance, where I get to feed off and finalise that dream. Trap those who speak in tongue; assume they have the power and the outcome will be done.

It had me in knots presenting the corrupt with a brand-new breed; no good deed intended. Where every challenge brought forth a reality check; It was part of a trend that will tempt me at every final. Preventing the corrupt from entering my realm. It had me in a spiral that was circulating.

It was feeding the decision that handed the deception. It was causing an effect and leading the corrupt to the wrong destination It was part of a mission, and a condition where the corrupts mission took me on vision, to break the silence. It had me hit back with violence.

All while they surrender all inhibitions. I go through hell, trying to make sense of what I did to redo another clue. It was part of a fate that had me step into the Abys. Trying to repeat a trace at the end of the race. The energy to repeat replace and follow up on a trend; that was part of a review.

It became part of my faith that broke the silence in the end. I hit a dead end back only to witness it was all in my head. The opportunity to clear the debt, became a threat. It landed me a role that forced me to bite the bullet and feed off the corrupt whole.

It handed me the inclusion, to belt the corrupt with an illusion. Then when the time come, release that beast; that forced me to repeat. It was part of a challenge where the corrupt ended and I could not surrender my anger; unless justice prevailed. Where I get to meet my maker before I sail.

I was about to lose my will, my presentation, and my skill. It handed me a violent interrogation to claim my thoughts and hit back with a final reservation. For that manifestation had me create another ride of a life time. Left to suffer in silence, just so the corrupt can override a side effect.

I was to hit with a run, fed off the outcome. Just to make do, with what I knew. Creating a cancelation to that manifestation, had me proving the corrupt were using me by denying and hitting me with an absence to that trace; that forced me off the race.

It was presenting me with a key, leading me to a destination that faced me with a curse that had me come first. It gave me a chance to hit back in advance. So, he who knew can finalise another review forcing me to face a fact so can get through. I had to finalise and fact and get back on track.

It was part of a trace to that case, that had me release that beast. It was forcing me to redo and accomplish another review. It was presenting the corrupt with a dead end at the end of the race. where I get in and feed off the energy that had me force to redo and follow up on another review.

I had to overcome another outcome, where I was out for revenge. I had to walk into a trace face a fear, trap that trend feed off the energy and start again. That triumph, that created the piece ended in tragedy, because the corrupt saw me as a curse, they took me in and fed off me from within.

I was torn every direction, left to suffer in silence; so, the corrupt can continue to ride the wave. I had to return and hit with an alluring effect. For an alliance had created a defect and the only way I could return was press replay, a test that had me face a trace that was pending and never ending.

A trend that forced me off the edge, revealed what I thought was part of the last resort. All so I return for another pledge, hitting an end that had me starting again. It was to cause an effect feed off the defect, then without delay press delete and follow up on a game strengthen me again.

I had spirit, it handed me the upper hand to get back on track; feeding off the outcome. It forced me to reveal, revive, and follow up on another dive. It had me entering the realm of those who erase, creating a message that will hand me the outcome; I need to feed off that debris.

I was taught a lesson, left to release and follow up on a feast. Trapping those who assume they could return and consume. Facing a trend in the end of that test, had Recreated a follow up. Just to prove to me I hit a dead end. The outcome that stated the fact, faced me with a case; releasing the beast.

It was merely part of a final degree. A challenge that will hand me the results I needed to cut corners. Where the corrupts method had me up close and personal, leaving them suffering in silence. All while I catch up succeed facing another trial an error; a trace that will hand me a terror.

The curse I need to rehearse; reversed and I come first. It had me face another trace, that brought me forth. A conclusion that will hand me the edge of reason. All While I give in and feed off the trace that served me well from within. I had to follow up on a trend that took me in.

It had me feed off the challenge from within. I was moving forward too little too late. The next final request had me face a trace. It took me in a broke the silence that had me present the corrupt with a final. I became transparent and everyone who knew; wanted to screw me right through.

Where I get in, face them with a trend and let them in. A knowing, if they repeat the old, the new will break through; breaking that demonic spirit. A challenge that had hit back with ease, it caused an effect and faced me with a trace that served me a case kicking a fuss; tracing that trend.

It restored my energy, took me in failed me from within and had me play a foolish game. All so I can catch up and remain the same, it led me to believe the lie was the truth. Only to witness the lie was the truth, but he who was meant to be, was taken away from me.

He never showed up, he shut me out, shut me up, and stabbed me in the back. I was taken for a fool pushed off track, then when the time come, cleared the air, and faced another outcome. It was purely to get back on track; it forced me to overlay connect to wrong and replay.

I had given it a deep thought, so when I caught up, it will hand me the power to create a war. Where in the end the corrupts final regard, will hand them a dead end. Creating a force that will hit back with remorse. So, when I catch up, I could force my way in; trapping the corrupts method.

It had me face another trace, create, an impact I can relate too. So, when I got in, I won a new inning. It had me face another fight, feed off the trace that restored my energy and created a trend; that had me replace another dead end. I had to curse that verse, that had me come first.

In the end of that verse, there was a presentation that handed me an evaluation. It was part of a past test that had handled the whole situation with a force that caused an effect. It broke the silence and presented me with a curse that cannot be rehearsed because every trace served me well.

I was taught a lesson, too little too late, a proposition put me through hell. It handed me the leisure that took me on a journey that presented me with pleasure. It gave me a first and last, everlasting approach a key that caused an effect and broke every rule; so, I lose my thought pattern.

The vision that handed me a proposition. It was giving me the power to undo and devour. For that trial the error forced me to redo and claim another review. It led me towards a terror, that caused an effect and broke the silence and had me resurrect to the next defect.

I had to conclude that my journey; embracing another trial and error. I had to undo and look forward to another review. I was forced to feed off the edge, look for answers that never come too. Break the silence that had me look forward to what I thought was the last resort.

It was part of a trial and error, a foundation that brought me terror. I was taught a lesson left to redo; so, when I catch up feed off the clue. With out a final review, I had to feed off the test that led me process another progression to that terrible act of kindness; that had me fail every quest.

I was to face another trace, look forward not back. Because every trace trapped me in the middle of the race. I was facing deception to that manifestation that grabbed me and put me forward straight into a faith less likely for me to fail and more likely for me to prevail.

It had me face another case, giving me the power to undo and devour. I was to feed off the trace that had me return and replace. I was given a reason to hit back with treason. It was forcing me to replace the old the new and the forthcoming review. A cause I could not face unless I repeated it.

It was handing me the resolution to that individual restitution; causing an effect. Led towards a destination that forced me of the edge; trapped in the middle of that pledge. Repeating a new tread. Giving me the power to undo and prepare myself for one more over cast.

A final review to refine that trial and error, it had me delaying another dilemma. I was Drenching in an emotional roller coaster of sorrow. Wasting valuable time trying to declare and decline a final review, a faith less likely to embrace the case. Had come to fruition; and gone through the mission.

I was given a reason to hit back with treason. For whatever caused the effects case closed. It was handing me a defect. A chance to heave in advance, forcing me to replace repeat and hand the corrupt a chance to press delete. It caused an effect and broke the silence so I can resurrect.

For that reason, I hit back with treason, it was part of a final request. It handed me a final review forcing me to repeat replace and follow up on another case. So, when I reached my peak, the trace becomes an abundant line of events. It caused an effect, deleted and delayed a shred in the end.

The trend became meek, the journey obsolete. It gave me a second chance to get back on track and delete. I had my chance to undo that review, release that beast and case close that trend that served me well in the end. It gave me a task to get back on track; a presentation that had me investigated.

It was part of a personal vendetta, that had me release and find peace. I had to replace that trace that had me stalling. It forced to erase, a follow up on a condition that had me release a vision to that competition. The entrance was cursed; the drama was reversed; I reserved for a curse.

For the trace was served, it gave me a condition that forced me off the edge. It was part of a trend that served me well it gave me a final feast it led me towards an ending that was pending and a challenge that was never ending. Where the only thing that created the piece had me erase the case.

I was served well at the end of the race; it had me forced to enter the corrupts realm and entertain them through hell. I was given a reason to replace the old, refine the new catch up and follow up on another review. I had to come first and create a piece and follow up on a feast that served me well.

I was left to undo and follow up on a review; so, when I caught up, I could screw them too. For the energy that faced me had me causing effects. It served me well and trapped me while I went through hell. It gave me a second chance to belt the corrupt in advance.

So, when I hit my mile stone, I could embrace the case. condition the mission and feed off the trace. It took me on a temporary hold up. Repeating a competition, all while I get back on track facing a dead end at the end of the mission. It presented the corrupt with a final review.

A second chance to hit back with denial, created a follow up to that trial. It had me face another curse at the end of that first and last verse. It forced the corrupt to catch up and create a follow up to the next trace. A trend that will help me face another foreclosure in the end.

A piece that broke the silence took me in; followed up on a clue. Letting the corrupt know, I was about to let the corrupt go. Releasing that demon that forced me to replace, redo, and follow up on another review. Where I get in feed off the trace that served me well at the end of that spell.

I was so tied up in knots, trying to catch up, so when I reached my potential the energy that served me wrong handed me a clue. It presented me with a case. that served me well; at the end of the race. So, when the time come, I could kill time freeing myself for a trace that served me hell.

CHAPTER 9

◆◆◆

WHEN THE CORRUPT RETURN FOR A REPEAT, KILLING TIME

I was taught a lesson left to retrieve, follow up on a new key. It forced me to give in give up then when the time come feed off the corrupt. The follow up to the next review had me on the edge trapped ready to give in and feed off the trace that had me face another trend.

I had a conclusion to that manifestation; forced me off the edge, straight into a demolition. Denying the corrupt access was the only way I could repeat and lead them astray. I was put in a position that had me hitting a final competition. Left to undo and release that demon, at the end of the mission.

For every time I was causing an effect, I was left picking

up the pieces; that had me torn. For what I knew and what was to come through was a true manipulation to that manifestation. I was left torn from that threat. I was taught a lesson left to entrap a trip down; a memorial park of regret.

Where the corrupt took me in, put me on a wild goose chase. Looking south, wasting valuable time feeding the trace, that had me on the edge. It had me trapped in the middle of a forthcoming riddle. I was left silent, nothing positive to say put in a position worse than the mission.

It had me questioning the motives of the corrupt. It was forcing me to hit back and create a Dynasty of hate instead of love. I was hunting for a feast, left to repeat reminisce, catch up, and feed off the bliss. It had me facing a trend kicking a fuss in the end. So, when I catch up, I could redo another cut.

Replace, a case finalising the trace, at the end of the race. Because they felt the energy subside, it had me on the run, hitting a rebound. Then attempt to coverup a trace at the end of the race. It was surrounding me with a curse, causing an effect, it brought me forward so I can resurrect.

It had me leaping bounds, hitting glory, waiting for the trace to erase. It gave me a return for another race. It had me feel defeat at every dive, defying every odd; suffering from within. In the end of that debt, there was a second trial; a threat that will hand me denial.

It had me face another trace, warning me that I was on

the edge. I was dragging my feet, leading the corrupt towards another trace at the end of the race. The decision to hit me at every disposal became a mission; causing an effect creating a defect.

Warning me I was hit with the edge of reason. It restored my energy giving me the impression the trace was part of a diversion. It gave me permission to hit back, feed off the trend, and trap the corrupt until the end. Where at every disposal I was given a reason to hit back with treason.

Because I found my way in, I was warned of what was to come; after that win. I honestly believed I would not been affected and every trace will serve me well and I will reach my peak resurrecting from that hell. I was hitting a hold up, all while I follow up on a trace at the end of that haste.

It handed me the evolution, I needed to get in. It had me finalising that win, giving the corrupt a dead end at the end of that terrible act of kindness. It had me face another warning, so when I hit the end of that trend the only troubles; was the challenge that hit me with a finally; I could face.

Ready and willing to release final feast, it had me forced to hit back with remorse. I was given a reason to praise he who held me hostage along the way. I was being forced to hit back with remorse it had denied me access at every cause. It had me face another trace and reap a reward.

I had to catch up and finalise that test, that had me

face another request. Because the trend was beginning to look like a lie; I hit a dead end. The truth was nothing but a final laugh because the corrupt could undo another review. I was given a trace that forced me to erase that trend.

I was given an entrance about to lose with a vengeance. There was no availability to the corrupts final ecstasy. It was just a challenge to hit me with vulnerability. I was about to be hit with an entrance to that performance. It was giving me the notion; I was about to harm, my emotions.

It was part of a conspiracy, that caused an effect. It had me sit in admin, waiting for the trace to hit a dead end and hand me grace. Where I was given a reason to hit back with treason. A liability to that extension, became an expense. I had finalised that trend and fail the corrupt in the end.

It became my way of creating, what I thought was; the last resort. A challenge to bring forth a new reality, where I was given a reason to hit back with treason. For the corrupts challenge was unbearable. I had to refine, catch up, and finalise that energy with a reason.

All so I can feed off the trace that had me break the silence at the end of the race. It was part of a past hint, that trapped me in the end. It was leaving me stagnant to a development that was not meant to be at that moment. It was part of suggestion that was meant to happen in due time.

Little did I know he who knew lured me into his world.

He had stolen my key, back when I was creating the piece. It had me facing another feast. I was taken for a ride straight into a dive, where I hot a hollow shallow barrier between here there and everywhere.

Where I falling into the deep, waiting for the moment to repeat. I had to reclaim and follow up on another game. Feeding off the trace, that served me well at the end of that trend. It had me face another dead end. It created an anomaly, just to catch up; leaving me stunned and stranded.

It was landing a role where I was living a lie. So, the corrupt can give in and belt me from within. Anxiety and regret, took me on a path where every trace had me face another case. It left me to continue on my path; carrying a burden. A follow up towards a journey that had me repeat.

Finalising that method that stirred the pot, where it had me, fighting for my life. I was masking taped, tied in knots, and left to face another day. Reminding myself the dream was part of a gamble just to release that beast that forced me off the edge; straighten into a failed attempt.

A debt that left me frail at the end of that trail. It was part of a key that had me release that beast that served me an anomaly. There was no faith in that journey, it was all part of a trick that took its toll and forced me to hit back with a warning. I was handed a role and left to delve into a challenge.

It forced me to redo and accomplish a goal; at every

review. A task that ended in an uncompromising position. I had been taken for a ride forced to hit back and follow up on a journey that had me face another trace trending to be pending while the corrupt surrender at every measure.

It took me on a pathway that led me towards a journey, that had me feed off the trace that forced me to replace another trend in the end. Where every event had me face another tradition. It was part of a travesty that made me see I was never truly happy.

Whatever come my way, there had to be a player who will harm me along the way. There was always an ulterior motive that will sting me. It would not only leave me stunned but stung trying to get of that outcome. It was turning heads, testing my patience; tuning in for another inning.

I get in, heave at every threat, case every trace. Then take the initiative terrorise a hiding that served me a goal. Giving me the indication I fell into a faith less likely for me to succeed. More likely for me to sail as the corrupt prevail. It served me well presenting me with a key; handing me unity.

Entering a curse, I could reverse had me rehearse. Feeding of a good deed that served me first. I get in, break the system that led, me towards a journey that forced me off the edge. Straight towards a common ground. Facing me at the end of that trend; regaining conscious awareness again.

It was part of a majestic tradition, that served me a

proposition. It was handing me the entertainment I needed to reclaim and follow up on a new game. It gave me a sense of reality hitting me with technicality. Approaching an ending to that mission that was meant to be everlasting.

It was part of a past test, that had me forced to regress and digest. For what I thought was the last resort, handed me the exception to that redemption that forced me to hit back with a final interrogation. I was holding on to a force that had me face another trace.

It had me cave in on the concept and follow up on a trend. It faced me with a dead end, where I was made a sole provider in the end of that test that had me cause an effect. For he who knew could lavish in luxury and outdo me and follow up on another review.

For the energy that took me in warned me I hit a free ride. It led me towards a test, that took me in and finalised that method so I can win another inning. It had me fast forward towards a manifestation that led me inwards. Dropping a clue and feeding off the temperament.

It had me skip and escape another tradition; at the end of that interrogation. Warning me I had no freedom, to follow up on nor even face another trace; at the end of that forthcoming race. Whatever was pending had me face another final ending. A trend that left me spellbound.

I was dreaming of what could be, instead of creating a trace; that will hand me a case. In the end whatever was meant to come to fruition, there was no competition. For the journey was on hold; only for one mission. I had no control or the connection what I had was a trick and a trace.

The end result was unprecedented. It had faced me with a final, where every momentum carried a review. The only thing holding me up, was the one thing that broke the corrupt. It was to hand them a chance to clear the air, case that trace. Force that feast and praise that test that released peace.

The drama that had me release the beast, took me on a journey that had me find peace. I could not undo that review, I was too busy trying to cancel out a break, that had me face another trace. It was forcing me to embark on a feast. A trend that was pending, had me repeat the never-ending.

It handed me a pretentious outlook, a test that would provide me with a trial and error. A final faith at the end of that tremor. I was terrorised from the start until the end and the only thing that gave me the power to win was the trace that served me well from within.

I needed to release that trace that served me well at the end of the race. An ending, that was pending created a challenge that was never ending. I had no chance in hell in releasing that beast that forced me to release, it had me process a freak show. I had to break cycle with a warning.

It was part of a challenge that caused an effect. It gave

me a second chance to hit back in advance. It had me reaping a reward and trapping those who undo. It had me stepping into a challenge that served me well and presented me with ongoing clue. It gave me a chance to hit back in advance.

A challenge that gave in, handed me a final a feast at every arrival. I was served well and given a chance to advocate a task in advance. I was to follow up on a trace that served me well, at the end of the race. It was part of a personal endeavour that trapped me and had me case close a vendetta.

It returned faced me, with a given chance to save my soul and embrace that final. Because I was let down many times, the lesson I was taught had me fight back and embrace another trace. A given reason to hit back with treason. Where I was led on and given a mistake that became erratic.

A degree of energy that gave me pleasure, had me presenting the corrupt with a dead end. Where I was on the mend, waiting for them to release that beast. It forced me to re-enter repeat then surrender leaving the corrupt failing every test on request. A method that had changed the trace.

All so I can progress, I had to redo another review, where every momentum handed me an expense. It served me a trace at the end of that trend. It served me well at every destination. I was given a reason to hit back with a feast. It forced me to repeat and gave me a chance to face that test.

The corrupt had me analyse every move; it gave me a chance to hit back in advance. I had to finalise that method, hand them a reason to break their spirit while I feed off the system. I was given a time out, a chance to hit the corrupt with doubt. Just before I was given a reason to change the system.

I was forced to rearrange to hit back with a development that pushed me off track. Having me follow up on a review. For the spread had me facing a yearning. I was left to repeat, rebel and even encourage the corrupt to put me through hell. Just to save he who knew and he who had a clue.

It was preparing me for one more review. I was given a free ride that had me override and subside. The challenges that took me in ha me face another preparation; that broke the silence from within. I was in-between two worlds he who knew and he who had a clue.

Every time I hit the end of that trend, the valid response became invalid. Where the energy that served me, presented me with a clue, it broke the silence and faced me with a review. Every trace gave me the power to erase. It had me creating a return, troubling me in the end of that turn.

For every challenge had me forced to hit back with remorse. I was given a reason to hit back with treason, a trace that led me to believe that every momentum was too hard to reprieve. I was losing faith that had me reset then repeat; rebelling against those who press delete.

I was on the wrong path, taken out of my comfort zone. It led me to believe that my dream was not a reality, in fact it was part of a trap to push me off track. It had me working towards a raw restoration to the corrupts manifestation. It was part of a destination, where the trace was corrupt.

It became part of a travel; less taken. I was taught a lesson; left to respond I was hit with a final manifestation that had me erase that next common denomination. Just to keep myself forsaken. I put on righteous path surrounded dimwits. Light headed individuals who had no energy to break.

What they had was another, working outbound. Under the raider telling them how to respond. It was disheartening because I was stuck fighting a case that ended in tragedy. It gave me a second chance to follow up on a clue and face me with another review. I was overloaded with information.

It gave the corrupt a failure to launch and I chance to belt them in advance. It had me at the end of that trend that had me override that method the evaluation to step into the corrupts final evaluation. I had to revive another delegation to the next investigation.

I was given a chance to hit back with a trace, that served me well. It presented with a condition that forced me to hit back with curse, that had me revealing a first. I had to fight back that verse that served me wonders and help me come first. It had me revealing a violation to that manifestation.

I was given a chance to hit in advance. Using the method that handed me switched on. It was part of a review that had me constantly on the path of reaping a reward. It had me feeding off the trend that had me face a dead-end. I was served a challenge, that forced the corrupt to evolve.

It gave me a second chance to dive into a path; that had me face another bad day. I was on the trail to create a challenge; that was not meant to last. It had me deleting and delaying a trace, to that case that had tormented me. About to repeat, replace, handing me a review; a need to pull through.

I was forced to repeat, give in and follow up on a trace. An ending to that case that had been pending. It had me finalise that review, catch up and face that chaos at the end of that trend. It forced the corrupt to repeat, and a chance for I return and reassure them; it was not my turn.

An impression had me on the edge, it had me pressing delete. All while walking barefoot on egg shells, with a given, wasting valuable time handing me entertainment. It forced me to hit back and feed off the corrupt. All so I can get back on track; denying them access at the end of that light.

I was about to reminisce on a past test; it had me facing that finally. It was part of a case cancelling that test that had me digress. I was off the edge straight off the bat, about to process my progress. Only to witness I was strutting yet, straight into a ditch, facing a development; pausing an effect.

It had me on the edge, warned of what was to come that outcome. It was part of a finally, that had me hit a symmetry. A presentation that warned me. Every test I had entered created a personality trait. It had many not wanting to connect with me; because I was not that easy.

CHAPTER 10

◆ ◆ ◆

KILLING TIME WAS THE ONLY WAY I COULD FORESEE

It had me hitting the seven wonders of the world. Just to catch up and face another personal vendetta. One that will hand me a trace at the end of that case. It caused an effect and prepared me for a defect. Handing the corrupt debris at the end of the race.

I was taught a lesson, time after time. It left me to repeat, stepped into a world of my own. It helped me get through force my way in face another trace. Then when the corrupt lease expect it cease the day. It took me on a trace that served me well at the end of the race.

Then when I was on the move and the time come. It handed them a refusal to that rebuttal. Where I get in and face another trace at the end of that case. For that challenge gave me a free ride to the other side. It had me competing with he who had it in for me.

Trying my luck to face another trace, at the end of the race was part of a talent that gave me a presentation forcing me to hit back with a final investigation. For that appraisal had me on the edge facing what I thought was the last resort. An attempt to pass another case to that trace.

It gave me the power to violate an entrance to that deception that forced me to hit back with a violation. For I was given a chance to hit an extension to that redemption at every disposal. Where I get in finalise that ending, handing me the upper hand to that manifestation that created the piece.

It had me pending for another final. A reminder the edge of reason had me pledge for a finally. It warned me I was heading towards a journey that presented me with a gift. It was part of a deception to that redemption that caused an effect and handed me the road; towards manifestation.

Meanwhile catch the corrupt at the end of the race, feed off the trace. Then when I least expect it cast a spell giving the corrupt hell. I was to cause an effect, create a piece and face that demon who was handing me that random key. The one I needed to release that beast that forced me to repeat.

They were stalling, facing me at every wrong move. Presenting me with a test that had me face a contest. Where I was given a challenge that created the piece. It had me step forward and break the corrupts silence from within. An added conquest to that test that had me repeat an allegation.

I had to follow up on a review feed off the concept and create an over view. It was part of a trend that served me well in the end. It gave me a second chance to belt the corrupt in advance just to get glimpse of another future event. For that trend that had me face a dead-end.

It was part of a faith less likely to retaliate. Because the journey was presenting me with a key. I hit the end of my path ready to break the cycle and rebuild a new wrath. A challenge that had me repeat a situation; followed up on another destination. Where my creativity, took over that energy.

It was part of a trace that had me feed off the concept. All so I can clear the air and face another demon. It had me grieve, surrender and reprieve just to see the corrupt succeed. It forced me off the edge straight into a curse, where I give in and finalise that tenderness from within.

It had me give up, then try my luck belting the corrupt. It was the one thing that served me well from within. It was creating a war, in the corrupts mission once more. So, when I reach pinnacle the only thing that had me fail, was the journey. It gave me the power to get in and win an inning.

The incantation to manifestation warned me, I had no condition; to validate the competition. I needed to reap a reward, that was stalling, purely to feed off my dynasty. It had me face another trend in the end of that test. Forcing me to review a follow up on another clue.

The corrupt handed me an opportunity to enter their realm. Force my way in and face another doom from within. A trace at the end of that case became expensive. Not only I was losing money but my light dimmed. I could not stand to indulge in a rage. Several individuals were belting me from within.

As I rose above and beyond feeding off the concord. The unity to the corrupts force, became intolerable, to my faith. It had me repeat, rebel feed off the trace; putting me through hell. I fell and was given an early rise, just to get in and finalise the impact that had me facing there, evil twin.

It held me up, and gave me a chance to fight back in advance. Forced to erase that case, so when I reach the end of my road; the only thing that held me back was the morose. Led on, while stepping into a warning; it made the corrupt strong. In the middle of a curse that led me towards hell.

It had me facing another challenge, creating a faith that had me win. I was forced to repeat face another case, feeding off the energy that finalised me at every trend in the end of the race. When I entered that era, I was not expecting that trace to belt me at the end of the race.

I failed, when I reached my peak, because I was held

hostage by the system. It left me to fight a lost cause. When I hit the end of that trend, the only thing that had me follow through; was the dream, that served me well at the end of that scheme. Handing me an expense not worth the troubles.

Because I was so caught up in trying to catch the corrupt. It caused a lot of negative effect; I was taught a lesson trapped in the middle of a trace. It broke the silence and the trend in the end. I was forced to repeat press delete; delaying another bad day. All so I can continue on my journey.

I was so caught up in a trace, that had me forget to repeat, and delete; what I was meant to delay. Because I was left pushing forward, I was led towards the wrong direction. I found myself lined up for a dead end in the end of that resurrection. Where I found a way to press replay; no more delay.

I had to re-enter process the game; hitting the corrupts method all the way. So much happened in such a short amount of time I could not release find peace nor even state a fact, for I was hit in the end facing a dead-end. Where the only thing that gave in, was the challenge that forced me to win.

I had to trace, what I assumed was the end of one bad day. A passageway towards the beginning of a brand-new day. That curse that had me rehearse for another first, caved in on me and handed me the edge of reason. I had to follow up on another case, creating a war in the corrupts peace.

All so I can condition the mission and find peace. I entered a presentation that had me hitting the beginning of a new inning. I was left to take the wrong move, feed off the trace, face a case, cause an effect, and break the cycle in between. Just so I can finalise that wisdom, that had me awakened.

Where the silence, became violent and my faith, was handing me the evolution to return for one more restitution. For the corrupts test, at the end of that request; had me face another trace. All so I can resurrect towards the next final threat. I entered that realm with a competition.

It was part of a condition, where the mission became part of a restitution; to the corrupts finally. I get in, cause an effect reap a reward feed off the energy that had me face another trace at the end of the race. I had to enter the corrupts face another trace and heave at the corrupts expense.

I was taught a lesson, left to repeat a given. Just to finalise that trend, that had me merge, with those who had no freedom; to embrace another case. I managed to enter the corrupts realm, and exit with the same imperative game. So, when I reach my foreseeable, pinnacle I could start again.

Where I get to end that trend; with a trace. I was served well, forced to face another upcoming spell. I had to get back on track and feed off the energy that had me fail and face another trend at the end of that forthcoming scale. Facing another final admission to that admiration.

It had me wait patiently for the corrupt to return and hit back with an extension to that redemption. I hit the end of that deception, trapped in the middle of a travesty. Warned of the energy that come to fruition. Fixing the end that test that had me hit a dead end the process the next progress.

For whatever reason come my way, it was the last thing that forced me to press replay. I had to replace a trace, curse the verse, condition the mission, and follow upon another competition. I was taught a lesson and left to breach the tradition; just to break the cycle that hit me at every arrival.

For that test that had me process and follow up on a contest. Forced to reclaim a new improved game. It gave me a chance to release that feast, that forced me to redo and accomplish a review. I was on the move, waiting for the corrupt to overpower; undo and finalise that trend.

It had me pretend giving me a second chance to belt the corrupts method in advance. Where I was given a reason to follow up on another mission. Just to release that beast that forced me to overcome another trace at the end of that case that had me on the run.

It had me repeating every trial, error, and an end to that terror. All so I can win another challenge from that deception that served me a well at every redemption. It was part of a well-deserved desire to release all inhibitions. Restore my energy cave in on the mission; and convey every competition.

For the way it came to be had me releasing another ongoing restoration to that manifestation. I had nowhere to go; I was nowhere near where I was meant to be. I had to rely on the corrupt to get by, then when the time come, release that beast. It had me fast-forward to the next feast.

I had to undo all the knots they put me through. The test was part of a quest, that had me retrieve another trace at the end of the race. I was forced to replace an ending that was pending. It had me tormenting the corrupt at every leisure pushing forward and creating a final dilemma

I was given a challenge, that had me face another review. It had me keeping it simple; all so I can skip that too. I had to refine and follow up on a theme, catch up, and finalise that trend that had me break the silence from within. It was causing effects; warned of the debt.

A given permission to release the beast was not part of the trace it was part of the corrupt chase. It had me warned waiting for the corrupt to challenge me with denial at the end of that trend. Where I had to get in and feed off the trace that served me well at the end of the race.

Warning me every competition, had an experience; that formed an alliance. It had me face another trace at the end of the race. It was warning me I hit the end of what I thought will bring forth unity, from that scrutiny. It had me facing another final delay, hitting the corrupt in the middle of a trial.

It was part of an error, that had me facing a dilemma. It had me on the edge, presenting the corrupt with a brand-new threat. The train of thought, had me face a case; it caused an effect and presented me with a map that had me trapped. Causing an effect and breaking the silence so I can resurrect.

Warning me once again, I was about to face a trap that had been pending. It had me forced to pretend, give the corrupt a final release, so I can embrace what I thought was an entrance to the next feast. Meanwhile try my luck to cancel out the corrupt, so I can get in and face that test.

A trace at the end of that trend, had led me towards a journey; that forced me off the edge. It became part of a string of events that had me starved of a feast. I was facing a cover up so the corrupt can continue to telly up. It was part of a trend break the corrupts spirit in the end.

All so I can release peace, from that allegation. It had me face another investigation. Where every challenge had me forced to hit back with remorse, I was stalked without air. I had to repair the damages that followed. It had me facing another trace at the end of the race.

It was warning me, it had me face a new fear, the one that served me well at the end of that ongoing spell. It gave me a second chance to break the cycle, at the end of that trend. It had me forced to hit back with remorse. All while I was given a reason to hit back with treason

I was warned of what was to come from that outcome. It had become part of an undeniable truth. A challenge that handed me face a trace, that served me well at the end of that race. I was given a response to that outcome. Where every trauma, forced me to hit back with an aroma.

Not only I was led to believe that the lie was true, but the corrupt fell for it too. Which made me out to be true, where they fell into hell forsaken test. trying to release a beast just to find peace. All while I get back on track and face my true reality. A dream that became a drama in-between.

It was the corrupts final review, where every feast became my freedom to release that beast. Because I was caught up in a lie the only thing that brought me forward was the energy that had me face another trace. An entrance to a journey, that hit back with a vengeance.

I was forced to face a trace, track down those who forced me off track. I was pushed towards a journey that had no restoration or given foundation. There was no final resort just a feast to break the corrupts silence and reframe the game. It was handing me the rise above and beyond.

All while I catch up and feed off the energy. Forced me to clean up the mess; breaking the silence nevertheless. It was to press delete handing me the choice I need to face another chase. I was to break that trend that had me forced to hit back and pretend.

Where I never get in or win another inning. Unless I gave in and gave the corrupt a chance to win. This time around the bitter taste in my mouth was all around. Not only I felt the trust unwind back then but I was cornered ready to break the trace and hand the corrupt a dead end.

It was part of a destruction, from past reification. It had me on the move, stepping into a trapped environment. Ready and willing to return and break the vibe, that served me a trace. Then when the test come to fruition, feed off the corrupt and break the cycle; at every proposition.

It had me break the trend at first glance. Repeating a trend in the end. It was waiting for me to return for one more key. So, when I return to repeat a new case, the only thing mission was the failed mission. A drama that served me well, handed me a final review; all while I go through hell.

I get in feed off the trend that had me break the cycle in the end. It had me face another trauma hit back with an everlasting haunt. So, when I catch up, I cause an effect hitting a deception and rise above the occasion. Breaking the corrupts silence and handing them a failed resurrection.

It was part of foundation that gave me the finals. It forced me to hit back and break the corrupts cycle. Where the trace had me break the end of that faith that was forcing me to break the cycle. All so I never fail another reception to that redemption. Where I had to play the game and restart again.

I had passion facing another mission. For there was no chance in hell of conditioning the vision. I had been feeding off the competition, hitting an individual, whom entered my realm, unwelcome. He took a challenge, and fell into my spell. Where I enter face a win catch a few waves and start again.

I had to pave my path, take another role; while feed off the passageway. I had to start anew phase so I do not lose my vision nor fall into a trap of failed proposition. It was part of my jurisdiction that handed me the reservation to get back on track and feed off the determination.

There was no third wheel, just a final given, just to hand me a proposal. It will face me when I hit the next feed. It handed me the involvement that bring me to my knees. For I needed to embrace another trace to that case For I had to release that beast, that caused an effect.

I was following up on a trend, facing a dead end. It was part of a presentation to break the silence and force my way in. I had to break the cycle for one more chance to face another trace. It had me feed off the energy that led me to release that beast. Haunted by the past at the end of that feast.

A dead end at the end of trend, had me face a trace. It was praising those who enter my realm assuming I was welcoming them in fact I was ready and willing to kick a fuss break the silence and feed off the trust. It had me face a cause an effect that had me reveal a follow up to the next test.

It was part of a final feast, handing me the equation; to that quality. Not the equality needed to return for a chance to repeat a new treat. All because there was no fair trial, just stepping into a trend. Forcing me to hit back and repeat a dead-end. Taken for a fool, and enforced with a new rule.

With no intention for rivalry; I was to hit back with reverse psychology. Whom ever invented that method had no chance in hell either of getting on honest answer. At the end of that trend there was a throwback a chance for me to corner the corrupt and get me back on track.

I had to follow up on a tradition just to catch a glimpse of the corrupts mission. I was on the edge breaking every competition. Just to get a glimpse of what the corrupt had installed for me. It was part of a trace that served me well and handed me an incursion to that invasion.

Added with an intrusion to that illusion. It was part interval investigation, that served me well. It forced me to reclaim another dial up to the game. It was gambling my troubled thought, letting me know the corrupt hit the last resort. I was on my way, creating a war in the end of that final score.

What an uproar, where every presentation handed me a confirmation. A challenge that forced me to override what I thought was the last resort. For all I knew I hit a hold up and it had me that I was sitting pretty warned of what was to come from that outcome.

I caught up, and caught the corrupt. They were stepping boundaries hitting me with a challenge that will serve me an ending; no longer pending. Because the trace became true and the challenge released an endorphin that served me a clue. It handed me a chance to put the corrupt through hell.

Leaving them suffering in silence, feeding off the concept. I was led astray; it was facing me with a trace that took me on a journey; that had me undo; a review. I was handed a challenge that served me well. It caused an effect trapped me in the middle of a defect. Defending that dishonour.

So, when I reach my pinnacle, I could regain my conscious awareness again. I hit a hold up, ready to lash out at he who knew and wanted to clear the air. All by hunting me down with a conspiracy. For He was feeding off me was basically part of a trend that had me repeat a feast.

The train of thought that had me break the cycle and refine to the last recital. It had me repeat and challenge the corrupts method so I can press delete. For went back and forth back with a curse I could reverse. All I had to do was come forward and follow up on a trend.

It had me break the silence, instantly the corrupt loss their patience. Trying to hit me run and have me come to terms with the outcome. I had to pretend that the energy that taught me a lesson also brought me forward. It handed me a clue, fast-forwarding to the next overview.

It gave me a chance to return and beat the corrupt to the punch. For I was on the mend waiting for the mission to end. Even then I had no chance of repeating a dead-end. For the in the corrupts final endeavour had me feeding of the trace that served me well; presenting me with upcoming spell.

I had to face my fear and feed off the tracking that had me on set. On a one-track mind trying to clear the debt feed off the threat and accomplish another trap that served me well at the end of that forthcoming event that hit me; just before I hit a dead end.

ABOUT THE AUTHOR

Panagiota Makaronis

I am not going to boast about myself, my education my family values or views. In the end what can I say life is what it is and everyone has their presentation.

What level of education I have is not important here, the fact that I have lived through death threats, dead ends, and the Demons in my head is enough for me to say! Good reddens, to hard labour.

Life to me has been nothing but expectations with several disappointments, on the hope I get somewhere trusting people when they were meant to help me was another story.

Having said that how many times have I heard people say I am helping you, I let my guard down and it ends up a never-ending Drama a story. Where if I was to repeat will end up worse than the first.

Every goal I set for myself so far though, I have achieved. This book is one of them.

But at what expense I had to endure, just so I do not lose faith in myself and in Humanity along the way. Others who knew could not wait to trace test my patience on the hope they erase my passion and end the race before me.

Because I was living and breathing in a society full of competitors, trying to compete with me and entering my realm on the hope they can harm me for they assumed that had more man power than me.

My theory is just to prove that the world is Governed, not just by everyone you meet but also by the way you witness and see yourself. It plays a huge part when you are about to end one journey and rehearse a new path.

A journey I wish not to return and replay, if anything I just want to move forward not look back and return for revenge. Because my opponent lost a fight and could not harm me so he decided to alarm everyone on the hope they cave in on it start an Allianz and harm me that way.

It left cursing the ones who were reversing and rehearsing, just so they can return stir the pot and leave me stagnant. Stuck in a world of my own sitting in self-pity, no way out unless I fought my way out.

That created more war in my peace because those who knew me, knew me well, fighting back was the only way they can prevent going through hell.

In the end all it did, was make things worse, for they were making mountains out of mole hills. However, the interpretation was enough for me to see I was on the right track the risks I took was based on not losing my faith or myself because others were doubting me and create anomaly.

They were haunted by me and my spirit they could not handle my presence or wait to see where they could hit me and run with a dead-end challenge. The only way out was to hold on to my dream repeat rebel and hit with an All might Spell.

I had come across several individuals who could not wait to break my fighting spirit, constantly on the move of how to kill me and my spirit.

The constant rejection, let down from those stalkers who had nothing better to do then follow me everywhere. Enter my realm just before I am about to make it happen, it got to the point I was failing every test because of it.

Eventually I gave in it was evident, let my Guard down on the hope and the condition there abuse and their method return and back fires.

Having to pick myself up after being pushed straight of the edge from so called Evil! Family friends and Associates, those who I call the corrupt.

What can I say a job is a job well done, level of education is based on life lessons? Everyone has a theory and so do I. Whether you agree is another story to just agree to disagree.

All the studying I did gave me an outlook, a method and outcome where sometimes I look back and wish I never entered but again I would not be here if I didn't.

The theory of here see and speak no evil to me is a lesson lived and lesson learnt. A challenge I can honestly say, it was testing a trace for me to embrace look back and erase. As I face my fears overcome another failure to that feast that handed me release.

As I look ahead and watch my journey unfold with a story untold, it will become a final phase to the next part of my truth. A challenge that will give me the indication I was on my path a feast to release peace.

Everyone is looking for answers and the hope to live

through life with comfort passion and a reason without having to deal with treason.

My memoirs are based on my journey and life lessons, it is all in the book in the end only time will tell, what can I say will be me, keeping up with the programme my way.

Not the way they state it because I hesitate to wonder who is really saving me here. For in the end the matter of facts, is in my hands, because I am an individual. My thoughts are based on my life lessons and no one can challenge or change that.

I know every challenge has its presentation and what I see is I am about to shut one door and open another. Where my vision is no longer impaired and whatever is enlisted to get to this point is no longer in the back burner.

It belongs in my spirit it is mine I earned it! I am just messenger, just passing through the rest remains Ancient History added with a Mystery.

For those who read will understand read between the lines, because my point of view is a venture to next quest on hope I can make a difference to humanity for the next generation to read and interpret my vision as a composition not a competition!

Happy Reading!

BOOKS IN THIS SERIES

The Theatrical Melodia of my Life : Chronicle One

This book is based on my journey, the roller coaster I call life, my thought patterns, and my experiences. How I overcome so many turmoils, how I changed my perception, for it led me towards a destination that gave me tension.

Burning Crown Of Glory: Chronicle 25

I found myself in a position of questioning the motives of certain individuals. I was put in a situation, that had me forced to override, run hide, and return when needed

A Sinful Act Of Kindness From The Heart : Chronicle 24

Where one day at a time took a wrong turn, a least expected accident turned my life upside down. An unexpected nightmare. Exiting my comfort zone and hit with another dead end.

A Byway Chariot Awaits An Awakening Contingency: Chronicle 23

My Epistemology Theory, an Odyssey; My Bible! I swear by it! Where I fell into a trap and a trace that became part of a worrisome outcome.
Caught in a web of lies, taught me a lesson; left to suffer in between.

The Iconic Door To Peace My Souls Final Feast A True Awakening: Chronicle 22

A technicality to rectify a task from the past arose. It was to bring forth peace, torn at every trace an insightful memory; I was to replace a line up, for a belting. For what the corrupt did, just to speed up the process; was priceless.

Tetelestai Debt Paid In Full: Chronicle Xx

It is a one woman Comedy Show & I am the Comedian. I am to push forth, and preach my critical analysis. A tell-tale story, to catch up, and catch the corrupt red handed. For their mission, was to belt me to the ground. Just to hide a scam, a scheme a failed proposition in-between. A position to hand me joy, had come around.

www.ingramcontent.com/pod-product-compliance
Lightning Source LLC
Chambersburg PA
CBHW032051150426
43194CB00006B/487
9781764145770